OCT

MICHAEL CARDEW

a portrait

by

Garth Clark

published by
KODANSHA INTERNATIONAL
of
Tokyo, New York & San Francisco

This book is set in Monophoto Romulus; text printing by Komiyama Printing Company, Tokyo.
Four-colour offset, duotone, and monochrome offset plates by Toppan Printing Company.
Book design by Shigeo Katakura and Kim Schuefftan.

Distributed in the United States by Kodansha International/USA Ltd., through Harper & Row, Publishers, Inc., 10 East 53rd Street, New York, New York, 10022.

Published by Kodansha International Ltd., 2–12–21 Otowa, Bunkyo-ku, Tokyo 112 and Kodansha International/USA Ltd., 10 East 53rd Street, New York, New York 10022 and 44 Montgomery Street, San Francisco, California 94104.
Copyright © 1976 by Kodansha International Ltd.
LCC 76–9358
ISBN 0–87011–277–5
JBC 1072–785442–2361

First edition, 1976

CONTENTS

Acknowledgements 7

St. Ives and Before 9

Winchcombe 27

Achimota, Vumé, and Wenford Bridge 41

Abuja 55

Wenford and Beyond 79

In Perspective 93

Plates 113

Appendix

    Workshops 197

    "The Fatal Impact"   *Michael Cardew* 215

Bibliography 225

Index 227

PHOTO CREDITS

G.W.F. Ellis, p. 36 bottom
Kent Benson, p. 70
Ronn Hartviksen, p. 88 top, p. 108
Studio St. Ives, p. 19 top
Crafts Advisory Committee, London, Pls. 18, 23, 24

COLLECTIONS

Victoria and Albert Museum, London, Pls. 2, 14, 50, 57, p. 20 top
University College of Wales, Aberystywyth, Pls. 5, 6, 12, 13, 23
The British Council, Pls. 8, 10
Stoke-on-Trent Art Gallery and Museum, Pls. 9, 22
Bristol Art Gallery, Pl. 11
Cheltenham Art Gallery, Pl. 24

The majority of the remaining pieces included here are from the collections of Edward Bawden, Michael Cardew, Mariel Cardew, Ray Finch, William Ismay, Mary and Michael (Seamus) O'Brien, and Katherine Pleydell-Bouverie.

Acknowledgements

I am indebted to Michael Cardew for his co-operation, the hospitality of Wenford Bridge, and particularly for his notes on the workshops that I have so freely plagiarized. But the book would not have been completed without the enthusiasm of others: Mariel Cardew, Katherine Pleydell-Bouverie, William Ismay, David Coachworth, and the generosity of the Circulation Department of the Victoria & Albert Museum. I am grateful to all those who gave of their time and allowed me access to their pottery collections. Lastly I thank my wife, Lynne, who typed and administered behind the scenes. To her this book is fondly dedicated.

Garth Clark

Addlestead Farm, Surrey, 1976

ST. IVES AND BEFORE

Try to get that completeness of form — it is like a full moon.

— Bernard Leach

MICHAEL Cardew first became conscious of his "pot madness" in 1921, when he learned to throw at Fishley Holland's Braunton pottery. But the roots go back further—to half-remembered, half-imagined scenes of the white-bearded Edwin Beer Fishley bent over his wheel, watched by a silent and intent boy of eight who kicked his sister's shins when she arrived to drag him away for the journey home.

Cardew took the decision to become a potter at a time when the crafts were not fashionable and to work in clay was hardly even respectable. Because the arts and crafts movement had been largely a middle-class activity, it imposed a veneer of snobbery over its professed egalitarianism. Craft was all very well if practised by artists or at least poets.

This developed rapidly into a white-collar crafts movement, a fate that was particularly true of pottery. It was acceptable for a gentleman to design or involve himself in glaze chemistry, but the handling and throwing of the clay was considered to be the job of a skilled labourer. Given this climate, it is not surprising that at the turn of the century pottery attracted mainly failed artists and produced a relatively small number of really inspired ceramists.

Ceramics was rarely the first choice of the talented; the best potters from the late nineteenth and early twentieth century tended to arrive via a circumspect route. William de Morgan was attracted through his experiments in stained glass. Wallace Martin developed his love for clay from his work on terra cotta relief sculpture. Bernard Leach trained as an etcher, and William Staite Murray began as a painter. Cardew's commitment, however, was direct; he decided to work in clay very early in his life. Given his background and the social values of the time, his "pot madness" was a highly individualistic decision.

Arthur Cardew, Michael's father, was an enthusiastic collector of

Edwin Beer Fishley's work, and the buying visits to the pottery from the Cardew holiday home at Saunton were day-long family outings. They would walk to the end of the sands, hail a boatman from Appledore, and, if the tide was right, travel up to Fremington. In the amber Devon sunset they would return with the pick of the latest firing.

Fishley died in 1911, when Cardew was ten. But his presence remained at Saunton in the form of sturdy Devon jugs, deep oval baking dishes, and the rather overblown green and red glazed "art" pottery. The vigorous rural ware shaped Cardew's fondness for full-formed, functional pottery and was the most critical influence on his career.

Later, in 1936, when the contents of the home came up for sale, Cardew took care to rescue the domestic ware, a splendid plate with slip-trailed coat of arms, and the whimsical rhyme jugs. By then "Leach had taught me to be enlightened enough not to care what happened to the red and green pots for flowers".

Cardew came from the type of cultivated middle-class environment that had been the womb for most of the early twentieth century artist-potters. His mother, Alexandra, was the eldest daughter of G. W. Kitchin (Fellow of Christ Church, Oxford and Dean of Winchester and Durham), who numbered Lewis Carroll and John Ruskin amongst his Oxford friends. Arthur Cardew was a successful civil servant, and the family could afford to divide their time between the country home in Saunton and the house in Wimbledon. The latter was filled with "refined" china, to which Cardew took an early dislike.

Family life was close and stimulating in what he terms his "golden pre-war days". Amongst his purest recollections of childhood pleasures were the afternoons when the family quintet (Michael arriving at the clarinet after a process of elimination) spoke to each other through the music of Mozart and Haydn.

When the war came, he was too young and so missed the slaughter, but "it permeated the whole climate of those years of adolescence during which the future character is indelibly stamped, and then suddenly in 1918 gave place to an almost hysterical sense of relief and anticipation".

In 1919 it seemed that university was the logical place for a young man with so lively a mind. Cardew was awarded a scholarship and attended Oxford. It was then that his "pot-madness" began to develop and assume chronic proportions. Fishley's grandson Fishley Holland had set up a pottery at Braunton, and Cardew spent all of his free time learning to throw. Word of this came to the authorities at Oxford, and on his return from one of his throwing sessions he was called before his tutor and given an ultimatum, either cease potting or surrender the scholarship.

He agreed to give up pottery. It was the beginning of what was then known as "Greats" (ancient literature and philosophy), and Cardew felt that the classical philosophers would answer many of the questions that life posed at that time. "Of course they didn't . . . and only one half of me agreed to this terrible bargain."

His clandestine potting slowly developed again as the expectations in the "Greats" began to wane. At the Braunton workshop shortly before he left Oxford, Cardew noticed an article in the *Pottery Gazette* on two potters working at St. Ives, Bernard Leach and Shōji Hamada. Leach had started the pottery in 1920 after eleven years in Japan and China.

Leach had set off to Japan with the intention of teaching etching, which he had learned under Frank Brangwyn. But the teacher became a student of the quietist art of the Orient. In company with a group of young artists, writers, and actors, he attended a party in 1911 at which the main entertainment was a Raku firing. The guests were each given a bisqued pot to decorate. It was the sight of these pots emerging from their short baptism in the white heat of the kiln that inspired Leach to find a master who could teach him this art.

He was accepted by the sixth generation of the Kenzan tradition. For a year he daily attended "school" on the bare boards of the master's house in northern Tokyo. When he set up on his own, he was given the Kenzan *densho*. This is an honour that formalized the inheritance of the Kenzan title and the right to use the master's palette and glazes. And so both Leach and, soon afterwards, his close friend, the late Kenkichi Tomimoto, became the seventh Kenzans.

Leach returned to Britain partly to educate his children and "partly to set foot as a potter upon native soil and draw sustenance from it". He was accompanied by young Shōji Hamada, who had trained at the Tokyo Industrial College and the Kyoto Ceramic Testing Institute. Leach had met him a year or so previously at the home of the philosopher Sōetsu Yanagi.

Britain proved to be an inhospitable market for the pots that they produced at St. Ives. The collectors were just being weaned off the pre-Raphaelite painting on porcelain. The most popular art pottery of the time was produced by ceramists like Howson Taylor, who specialized in highly priced flambé ware, and Moorcroft, who produced decorated pots that were covered in a tight profusion of polychromatic floral ornament, drawn with a slip trailer and glazed in a cloissonist style.

Both men shared an interest in the more sophisticated oriental ceramics. At the time there was a good market for pottery that tended to imitate rather than interpret the quality of Chinese, Korean, and Japanese pottery. Charles Vyse and Reginald Wells were also popular artist-potters producing this genre of work in the 1920s.

By and large the term artist-potter was reserved for men like Howson Taylor, who mangaged small factories, designing pots and creating glaze effects. At the more extreme end of the spectrum, a demand was beginning to grow for the modern tin-glazed pottery by

Roger Fry's Omega Workshop, designed for the languid interiors of the Bloomsbury set, The Art Deco–Art Moderne movement on the continent was having its effect as well, and a taste was developing for crisp, machine shapes and cubistic designs in bright colours. What united this diverse output of "art pottery" is that, with the exception of the Omega Workshop, it was all object oriented; craft was dictated to by the unsatisfactory, amoral belief that any means justifies the end. And the end was a very pretentious Beautiful Pot with great value, with bland but flawless glaze. Forms tended towards a self-conscious modernity and, because they were so slavishly fashionable, enjoyed great popularity.

In this climate, the work of Leach and Hamada appeared to lack refinement and, above all, to lack colour, which was the criticism most often made about the work. "Now if you could develop some nice green and red glazes, I'm sure that your work would sell, Mr. Leach" was the frequent but misguided advice that he was offered in St. Ives. St. Ives itself had lost its glamour, which Leach and Barbara Hepworth were later to restore. The more adventurous artists had left. Virginia Woolf, D. H. Lawrence, and many of the other literary "names" had also moved away. What was left was a group of very conventional and academic artists painting conventional seas and academic sunsets. Leach was only admitted to the local arts society because he was an etcher. He could never have been accepted as a potter.

In January, 1923, Cardew was visiting Lake's pottery in Truro and decided that if there was a train he would go to St. Ives. There was, and late on a winter afternoon he climbed the Stennack to the Leach Pottery to be met by George Dunn, the studio labourer, and Shōji Hamada. He and Hamada walked the two miles to the Leach home at Carbis Bay, where he was introduced to Bernard, his wife, and the five children—three daughters, Michael, and twelve-year-old David.

Cardew ate a meal with the family, and on hearing that he was interested in working at the pottery, Bernard handed him a matt, paper-grey bowl with a decoration of incised fluting (see *A Potter's Book*, Pl. 2) and asked, "What do you make of that?"

"Of course I didn't make anything of it. I had seen and admired some Ts'u-chou pots that were beginning to appear in London. I had the sense to say nothing stupid. I felt myself then to be (and to an extent still am) a Western barbarian."

But Cardew did speak enthusiastically of English slipware, of Braunton, Fremington, and Fishley. Cardew believes that Leach accepted him for the sole reason that he was interested in reviving the English slipware tradition. However, Leach's recollection of Cardew's arrival in the introduction to *Pioneer Pottery* makes it seem more of a victory of enthusiasm: "He strode in, nose and brow straight, handsome as some young Greek god, eyes flashing blue, hair waving, gold, and within the hour announced that this was where he wanted to work."

Cardew worked for a short while at St. Ives in July, 1923, and then left for eight weeks in the Mediterranean, returning in November to find Hamada making preparations to leave and a new arrival from Japan, Tsuranosuke Matsubayashi. Cardew's exposure to Hamada was regrettably short. In those early days Hamada exhibited a gently Chinese quality in his pots. This appealed to Cardew immensely, since it coincided with a personal infatuation with the Orient. For a while he desperately sought for a Chinese quality in his work and even began to learn the Chinese language.

In visual terms, it was an unsuccessful attempt. Cardew worked ardently at trying to embody Sung purism in his work and eventually threw a lidded jar that he felt achieved this. Bernard walked into the shed, looked closely at the jar and said, "My goodness Michael, isn't it strange. Whatever you make is so extraordinarily English."

Soon after Cardew's arrival, Katherine (Beano) Pleydell-Bouverie

Edwin Beer Fishley (1830–1911) at the wheel, Fremington Pottery, Devon.

Plate by E. B. Fishley with slip-trailed coat of arms, ca. 1890. D. 40 cm.

Rhyme jug by E. B. Fishley, ca. 1910. H. 16 cm.

Standard Devon jug with galena-glazed neck, Fremington Pottery, ca. 1910. H. 16 cm.

St. Ives in 1923.

Cardew and Bernard Leach at Russell Workshops, Broadway, Worcestershire, in April, 1926, where they took part in an Easter exhibition of rural crafts and industries.

"Tree of Life" bowl by Bernard Leach, St. Ives, 1923.

Double jars by Shōji Hamada, ca. 1931. These jars later became inspiration for double jam pots by Cardew.

Chinese folk pot. Cardew adapted the sgraffito decoration on this type of Chinese peasant ware to English forms.

arrived in early 1924, to work for a year at the studio. Her impressions of the time and particularly of Cardew are vivid and charged with humour. Michael she remembers as "resembling one of those less archaic Kouroi that stand around the walls in Greek museums. He was subject to fits of temper that were extremely funny, appearing like thunder out of a clear sky and usually disappearing as suddenly. There was one occasion which I unhappily missed, when, moved by some unspecified irritation he solemnly threw twelve large bucklers into the pottery stream. After which, with equal solemnity, he walked into the stream and threw them out again. It is recorded that nobody laughed."

They were later joined by Norah Braden, whom Leach looked upon as one of his most gifted pupils. She was fresh from three years of drawing at the Royal College of Art, and her arrival at St. Ives was preceded with glowing references from Sir Henry Rothenstein. She brought an air of innocent irreverence to proceedings and voiced criticisms of Leach's work that none of the others would have dared.

From the start she showed her special aptitude for pottery. Braden was a perfectionist and hardly ever satisfied with her work. She broke up a good deal of her output, and few pieces remain in collections to evaluate her skill. From 1928 to 1936 she potted with Katherine Pleydell-Bouverie in Coleshill and then gave up pottery to teach.

Beano comments that while Matsubayashi's room in the town resembled that of a Victorian spinster, Michael's at the pottery was like something out of Mürgers' *Vie de Bohème*. Matsu was a great influence in Cardew's St. Ives days. He was the heir to the three-hundred-year tradition of the Asahi pottery outside of Kyoto, famous for its tea ceremony ware, and was in St. Ives to rebuild the Leach kiln, which had burnt out while preparing for a successful 1923 Bond Street exhibition. He built a small kiln to fire hand-made bricks and blocks for the new kiln, and Michael and the rest acted as supporting labour.

The artistry he lavished on the kiln never surfaced in his pots, which were "unbelievably awful", and Bernard never lost an opportunity to point this out to an impervious Matsu. In the evenings Matsu would lecture solemnly on ceramic technology, while Bernard questioned whether all this technical knowledge was necessary for making good pots.

"In a way," says Cardew, "it darn well isn't. My interest in technology came only by the sting of sheer necessity." So Cardew doodled on his notepad, drawing Devon harvest jugs while Matsu lectured. Luckily Beano approached the evenings more seriously and took copious notes. She wrote later, "The lectures were full of good sense, whenever it was possible to disentangle their remarkable English."

It was a pity that Cardew was not ready for the theory of ceramics at that stage, because Matsu probably knew as much as anyone at the time. The Japanese schools he had been to offered the finest technical training and were more in touch with the scientific German schools than the empirical Stoke-on-Trent.

Meals were a special time at the pottery. It was a time for interesting Japanese food and for talk. "Perhaps the best things about those meals were the plates and bowls that we used. There were some beautiful Ts'u-chou rice bowls which Leach had bought for a penny or two each at Shanghai or Hong Kong. They were rough but had infinite refinement in shape and in the slight, summary brush decorations. Eating from these exciting bowls, we went on to discuss how they were made, in metaphysical as well as technical terms."

"What I learned from Leach then I am only now beginning to appreciate," Cardew was to write twenty years later. One of the most valuable lessons he acquired was the supreme importance of shape and how much depended upon the subtle differences of form, even in such apparently simple things as plates and dishes. "He would show me an old slipware dish and say, 'Try and get that completeness of form—it is like a full moon.'"

The relationship was uneasy at first. Leach was too young to be a father and too old to be a brother. Moreover, he had been absent from Britain during ten crucial years, and Cardew tended to look upon him as a perfectly preserved Edwardian who had been delayed in a time machine. He recalls being hesitant to mention subjects such as Freud in case they would offend Leach.

Their bond was a common fascination with early English slipware. Cardew threw plates and bowls, and Leach would decorate them. They spent hours examining fragments of seventeenth century slipware dishes that were unearthed in Cornwall and discussing their quality.

It can be said that contact with Leach refined and gave voice to Cardew's aesthetic judgements. But the lessons learned were used to build up a personal philosophy and not to imitate that of Leach.

It is easy now for St. Ives to fall prey to romanticism through the tunnel of time. The period 1920–1926 was an extraordinarily fertile time in ceramic history. During this short space of time, three of the most significant names in modern pottery, Leach, Hamada, and Cardew worked there. In 1975 they have spent a collective total of 168 years as practising potters, and each has made unique contributions to the ceramic art and craft.

But the participants felt little of the excitement that has been retrospectively ascribed. St. Ives was admittedly not an entirely barren creative community. It did still attract a number of people from the arts. In particular, Cardew remembers Margaret Kennedy, with whom he had frightful arguments. Nonetheless, he read her book *Constant Nymph* and was amazed that "such an ordinary person could write such a wonderful book."

But for the most it was extremely hard work. The pottery was not an efficient unit in the first few years. Clay was a matter of day to day improvization, and there was never enough for their needs. Much of the time was spent in producing Raku pots, which was the only aspect of their output that received popular support. It was essentially a time of financial and technical frustration. In 1923 Leach ran into trouble with promised capital for the pottery, and it was only the high prices his work received in Japan that kept the studio afloat. His friends in Tokyo organized exhibitions there and sent the entire takings to St. Ives.

Firing the kiln was also a problem. There was little wood in St. Ives or anywhere else in western Cornwall, for that matter. It was only many years later that Leach finally converted to oil, but it taught Cardew an early lesson about the siting of a pottery.

There were, of course, the occasional catastrophes, and one that bears repeating was recorded by Beano's pen. "The first firing [of Matsubayashi's kiln] began, I remember, with a ceremonial offering of salt on the fire arch. And gradually, through the long day's slow stoking an atmosphere of tension developed that would have been quite suitable on a battlefield. The rate of firing increased, and the kiln grew hotter. So did we. There was a great deal of black smoke billowing out of the chimney, making an acrid fog in the shed. We got blacker. Night came, and in the flickering light of what Matsu called 'bro holes' and the crackle and flare of the logs in the fire mouth, we moved about like creatures out of the more sinister creations of Hieronymus Bosch."

"And then in the grey dawn, something began to go wrong. Matsu took out a spy brick, and as the wicked little flame that jumped out at him died down, peered into the incandescent kiln and let out a ghoulish roar. 'Oh-ho-ha-ha-hay-awful sings happen,' sang Matsu with every appearance of enjoyment, as a six foot bung of saggars leaned slowly forward and collapsed on to the front wall, blocking up the draft."

In 1926 Cardew began to reassess his position. He had begun to grow distant from the objectives at St. Ives, which were directed towards stoneware, for which he felt no responsive chord. Also his great physical energy could not find expression, since the pottery was run more as a studio than the rural workshop that he desired.

The time had come for Cardew to become his own man. An unhappy love affair brought matters to a head. Cardew felt it was simply too embarrassing to remain. He contacted the Butler family, who owned a farm at Greet near Winchcombe that included a pottery derelict since 1912. An offer had also come from Ireland to set him up in a pottery there. "I know that there are no 'ifs' in history, but I wonder what would have happened and where I would be now if I had accepted that offer."

But the Butlers replied immediately, accepting his offer, and for the rental of ten shillings per week he acquired a lease on the pottery. That year he moved to Winchcombe, where he was later to produce what Leach has called "the most honest English slipware since Thomas Toft".

M W. B. PATERSON REQUESTS THE HONO   .
OF YOUR COMPANY AT AN EXHIBITION ᴏꜰ

POTTERY

made and designed by

BERNARD LEACH
SHOJI HAMADA
MICHAEL CARDEW

Of the Leach Pottery, St. Ives, Cornwall

AT THE PATERSON GALLERY
5 OLD BOND STREET, W.1

From the 2nd to 13th June, inclusive

Open Daily—
10 a.m. to 1 p.m.   2 to 5 p.m.   Saturdays, 10 a.m. to 1 p.m.

WINCHCOMBE

Slip decorated pottery has invariably reflected the character
of the men making it—vigorous and intuitive and not marred
by self-consciousness or concern for transient fashion.

— Ronald C. Cooper
English Slipware Dishes 1650-1850

AT Winchcombe, Cardew succeeded in stopping the clock of history from 1926 to 1939, establishing a rural pottery workshop and reviving the English slipware tradition. There was no sense of altruism in this action. What he did was neither for posterity nor a deliberate act of revival. He simply consulted his own wishes and set about the long and difficult task of rendering the derelict pottery viable.

It is necessary at this stage to pause and examine the slipware tradition and the reasons for its decline. For the benefit of non-potters, slipware is the term used to describe handmade earthenware pottery that is decorated in a contrasting color with liquid clay of a creamy consistency, which is known as slip. This can be applied by brush, slip trailer, dipping, or pouring. Once applied it can be combed, feathered, or designs cut through (sgraffito).

Slip decoration has been traced back several thousand years. Fine examples of spiral and floral Minoan decoration appeared in Crete about 2000 B.C. It was used in Greek Attic ware, in Roman times, and flourished again in sixteenth century Italy. But the opening paragraph by Ronald Cooper in *English Slipware Dishes* says more about its raison d'être than any didactic history:

> Potters of every age and civilisation have made slip decorated ware in different characteristic styles. The mainstreams of traditional slipware developed in localities where people, for geographical or ethnological reasons shared common interests in agriculture or artisan life, and found clay, fuel and water in close proximity to their homes. In more remote parts of Europe slipware for household use is still being made and sold in village markets.
>
> Slip decorated pottery has invariably reflected the character of the men making it—vigorous and intuitive and not marred by selfconsciousness or concern for transient fashion.

Insofar as slipware is an English tradition, it dates back to the early seventeenth century. This was the time that the roots of post-medieval society began to flourish in the form of trade and import. During the period 1600 to 1640, vast quantities of continental slipware were imported from north Holland and Wanfried-an-der-Werra in Germany. The English potter soon took to this style of pottery decoration, but because he transposed it to traditional English forms inherited from Cisterian and Tudor Greenware, a purely indigenous slipware style had emerged by 1650.

The growth of slipware was encouraged by the arrival of efficient pottery merchants. Until then a potter's market was seldom more than a twenty-mile radius from his workshop. The wider market offered by the traders meant a growth in the "luxury" trade of decorated ware. Several pottery centres emerged in Derbyshire, Staffordshire, and in Devon. Stafforshire excelled at slipware and introduced feathering and marbled decoration. It is also famous for the genius of Thomas Toft, who marks a zenith in slipware artistry.

But the merchants also created a network that allowed the Burslem pottery centre in Staffordshire and Ticknall in Derbyshire to gain a stranglehold on midland pottery production from 1700 on. They also encouraged the errosive practice of piecework amongst the smaller potters, in which a potter was contracted to produce only one or two items. Thus, one pottery might make one- and two-pint jugs and another the larger ones. The merchant then collected these and distributed them.

By the end oof the eighteenth century the potter's craft had been demoralized and replaced by a "corporate" potter invented by industrial division of labour. Those craftsmen potters that survived made cheap undecorated redware (a name drawn from the rough earthenware clay that fired to a reddish brown). As Peter Brears points out in *The English Country Potter*, their survival depended upon the existence of a large, poorly paid community who were unable to afford the better quality and slightly more expensive industrial whiteware. Today the situation is totally reversed, and the craftsman potter now relies on a smaller market that is affluent enough to pay prices higher than those of industry.

From the 1800s onwards, the changes in life-styles and standards of living rapidly put potters out of business. For instance, from 1830 to 1870 the proportion of home-brewed beer dropped from 50 percent to $2\frac{1}{2}$ percent as a result of the 1830 Beer House Act. The market in brewing pots fell accordingly. The same trend showed in the sale of pancheons and barm pots for bread making as the number of bakeries grew. By 1850 the standard of living was rising by 10 percent a year, and the number who could not afford the marginally higher cost of whiteware grew few.

The potters who served a rural market fared better. Changes in life-style took longer to filter through, but in the countryside they, too, had to eventually face competition from Stoke-on-Trent. In order to survive, some turned to making hardware for buildings and agriculture. Others, like Fishley, prospered in the early twentieth century through keeping standards high, prices low, and producing a mixed range of domestic and art pottery. An indication of just how low prices were comes from Fishley Holland. In 1909 at Fremington the pottery was selling flower pots at three for a penny, giant washing pans at 1/6d (8 cents) and four-pint jugs at $3\frac{1}{2}$d (2 cents).

By 1900 only one hundred small potteries existed, and by the end of the depression, less than a dozen were left. Armed with more enthusiasm than capital, Cardew set about recreating the very type of pottery that the full weight of a society in transition was busy erasing.

It took two years to sort out the major problems of repairing the large updraught kiln and getting the pottery, which had been silent for twelve years, back into production. The pottery had supplied large washing pans, flowerpots, and pipes for the agricultural community. Luckily one of the potters who had worked there, Elijah Comfort, was still living in the area and working as an agricultural labourer. For the magnificent sum of £2 per week Cardew brought him back to the pottery, and a boy, Sidney Tustin, was taken on to turn the old man's wheel.

Elijah Comfort helped solve the problems of filling the kiln. It was 550 cubic feet and much too large for Cardew to handle alone. In the first firings there would be an island of saggars that contained the pots surrounded by Comfort's large washing pans on bungs of pan rings. On top would then go the flowerpots. In this way the kiln space was halved.

This continued for some time, but was ultimately not profitable. The large wash pans fetched a mere 4/6d (26 cents), while the market for flowerpots had been taken over by much larger and more specialized operations. So Comfort turned to making casseroles, or "stew pots", as they were then known. This he did well, although his forms were a trifle sleepy in shape. He refused to decorate, and so Cardew had to handle all Comfort's output as well as his own and concedes rather modestly that he "became quite good with the slip trailer".

There was no formal planning of a range of Winchcombe products. Items such as the very popular ten-inch dinner plates were made largely because Cardew needed some himself. Very little non-functional decorative pottery was produced, although Cardew did produce a limited number of vessels that were described as flower vases but that he prefers to call "storage jars". There were also his superb rose bowls, amongst the finest pieces he has made. An indication of the size of these bowls is that it would take a good four to five dozen roses to fill their ample forms.

For some time clay proved to be a major problem. Cardew first used red clay from Fremington and in desperation even used clay from a nearby brickworks. Also, the kiln would not fire high enough to eliminate severe porosity. "I was then still under the fallacy," he says, "that low temperatures were simpler to reach than high temeratures, which is simply not true. When one is firing earthenware one has to be 'spot-on'. Ten degrees above or below and one can have a failure, whereas with stoneware minor fluctuations in temperature are unimportant."

The 500-cubic-foot bottle kiln at Winchcombe Pottery (photographed in 1973).

Elijah Comfort, Charles Tustin, Cardew, and Sydney Tustin beside the horse-drawn pug mill, Winchcombe, 1934.

Charles Tustin and a close-up of the pug mill.

Cardew decorating slipware, Winchcombe, 1928.

Bernard Leach, Sōetsu Yanagi, Shōji Hamada, Henry Bergen, Norah Braden, Cardew, Katherine Pleydell-Bouverie's mother and sister, Coleshill, 1929.

Cardew, Mariel, and Seth, Winchcombe, 1935.

Building the Wenford Bridge kiln, 1939.

By 1931 most of the problems had been ironed out. A local source of clay was obtained, and Sidney Tustin's brother joined the pottery. A pug mill was installed and powered by a horse named Christmas—"because he took such a long time to come around". This was a year of the crash, but it proved to be one of Cardew's best years. Overall, the depression of the thirties made little impression on him, since he was living "very close to the ground".

In December, 1933, he married Mariel Russell and moved from the pottery loft to a small shack that he had constructed for £24. A year later Seth was born, to be followed soon after by Cornelius and Ennis. The life-style was primitive and frugal, but Mariel remembers the time with affection. "There must have been something of the primitive in me as well because I never looked upon the years at Winchcombe as being a hardship."

Cardew by now had begun to exhibit. The 1931 exhibition at the Royal Institute Galleries was followed in 1935 with his inclusion at the exhibition of English pottery at the Victoria and Albert Museum. But it was in 1938 at the Brygos Gallery in New Bond Street that he showed really exceptional earthenware. Two of his large rose bowls from this exhibition were bought by Henry Bergen and bequeathed to the Bristol and the Stoke-on-Trent (Hanley) museums.

But exhibitions were not the place to view Cardew's work at its best. Muriel Rose makes this point in *Artist Potters in England*, saying, "Cardew should not be assessed on solitary examples of his work: only the sight of the storage loft at Winchcombe after a firing, the wide floor covered with stacks of golden-brown dishes, jugs, mugs, cider jars, could give the idea of the full range and force of his ability." The kiln took thirty-five hundred to forty-five hundred pieces and was fired three to four times a year. In the later stages of his production, Cardew started to produce green-glazed ware and turned from the light amber-gold more towards a black and white slip.

There were failures as well as successes. "I often made mistakes because I was either too confident or too careless," he now says. "I only learned to be careful very slowly. Even today I am not careful enough for a potter. But, you know, carefulness can be a terrible virtue. It destroys thinking big, and one has the feeling that there is a certain bigness in recklessness."

Work dominated most but not all of Cardew's life at Winchcombe, as this extract from an Article in *Apollo* (1943) written by Ernest Marsh shows:

> Cardew's interest in all that pertains intimately to the full country life from which he draws so much inspiration is aptly shown by his love of and devotion to country folk-dancing, and his handsome agile figure has been a familiar feature of many a Gloucestershire, Wiltshire and Oxfordshire village hall and green, and on the floor of the Royal Albert Hall at the annual gatherings and international contests held regularly before the War. It is difficult to conceive of a more recreative pastime better suited to relax the tension and relieve the severe physical and mental strain imposed by the constant toil of throwing on the wheel and manipulation and wedging of the clay in its preparation for pottery use.

Severe mental and physical strain is a condition far removed from Cardew at the wheel. Katherine Pleydell-Bouverie says of him that he makes pots as a bird sings. She recalls another view of Cardew at play. He was persuaded to play the Angel in *Everyman*, which was being presented in a twelfth century barn near Coleshill: "He looked rather fine in Fra Angelica colours up in the loft; he shared the loft with a hen and announced the fact while he welcomed Everyman into heaven."

In 1936 a young man approached Cardew and asked to be taken on, because he "thought" he wanted to be a potter. Cardew told him to come back when he *knew* he wanted to be a potter. So Raymond Finch went to

London and for six months studied at the Central School of Arts and Crafts before presenting himself at Winchcombe again.

He proved to be good pupil and learned fast. "Cardew didn't actually teach," he recalls. "One learned partly by example, watching him closely at work and then attempting the same oneself. One also learned through fear." The "thunderstorms" had not yet mellowed when Finch joined the pottery, and the possibility of setting off one of these explosive charges made for diligent apprentices. "Loading the kiln was particularly difficult. Cardew would never tell one which pot he wanted next. One had to learn from experience and intuition. If that failed, then there would be a deafening roar of anger from the depths of the kiln."

By 1939 Finch had progressed sufficiently for Winchcombe to be left in his hands. For a long time Cardew had missed Cornwall; he spoke the language and was a Cornish Bard. Eager to return, he had been spending his weekends cycling about Cornwall looking for a small mill-house where he could set up a pottery. His searches were unsuccessful until one weekend he reached the St. Tudy area and heard that the Wenford Inn was up for sale.

"I really could not conceive what I was to do with an estate of such magnitude; it was three acres with a large house, stables, and a river containing salmon. What I really wanted was a hut in which I could make pots." But he bought the inn nonetheless for the sum of £500.

Looking back at his move from Winchcombe, Cardew now feels that it was more than the lure of Cornwall that prompted the decision. "I suppose it was a refusal to consolidate in a way. You see I had never really done anything more than just camp out at Winchcombe, first in the loft, then the hut, and later at a labourer's cottage."

"The business then required consolidation. This Ray Finch, to his everlasting credit, did superbly. But although I moved to Cornwall, we remained in partnership for some time." The earliest pottery notepaper at Wenford had the line "Also at Winchcombe Gloucestershire".

Also he had been through the depression. There were unemployment problems, and friends and acquaintances began to question what the social significance was of a person like Cardew. "Of course there was none, and I believed the argument that I should employ my talents for the common good of the people by designing for industry. So I wanted to work with Stoke-on-Trent and I wanted to experiment in other ways. . . . Oh, there were many things I preferred rather than getting down to the job of consolidating Winchcombe."

Mariel remembers Wenford as the time of real pioneering. There was no pottery shed, water had to be fetched from the river, and the kiln had yet to be built. In June, 1939, the kiln construction began, but three months later it was little above ground level due to the unsettled political and economic climate of the time. It was not completed until July, 1940.

The war made running the pottery almost impossible. Blackout restrictions alone were a terrible limitation when firing the kiln, and the local constabulary were not sympathetic to this strange left-wing radical in their midst. "My greatest fear was being fined for contravening one of the many wartime regulations. Because if I was fined, what would I pay the fine with? We had no money at that stage at all. All the money I possessed had gone into buying the inn. I couldn't get labour to help me run the pottery. Then on top of all that Ray ran into trouble, they called up both the Tustin men, and after only two glaze firings at Wenford, I had to return to Winchcombe from autumn of 1941 to June, 1942."

While at Winchcombe a letter arrived from the Colonial Office saying that Harry Davis, the pottery instructor Cardew had recommended for Achimota College on the Gold Coast, was leaving and could he recommend another replacement. No one was available except Cardew at that stage. Motivated more by the interest of earning a regular salary than any fascination with Africa, he put his name forward and was enthusiastically accepted in what he now calls "the greatest piece of miscasting of all time".

ACHIMOTA, VUMÉ, AND WENFORD BRIDGE

If (Staite) Murray stands for the most cloistered virtue amongst our potters, Cardew is the most racy of the soil.

— George Wingfield Digby
The Work of the Modern Potter in England

THE term Pottery Instructor gives no indication of the scale of the operation that was being planned and implemented at Achimota College near Accra. The school was the Eton of West Africa and boasted the only art college of any importance in that part of Africa. The man who had come up from South Africa to take control of the arts was a Russian, trained in Germany as a master-carver, H. V. Meyerowitz. He was an artist-craftsman of considerable vision and had a taste for grandiose projects.

Meyerowitz had trained in Germany at the time when the German crafts were under the influence of the William Morris movement and the ideals of the Ashbee Guilds. Hermann Muthesius and Henry Van de Velde encouraged a German expression of the movement under the patronage of the Grand Duke Ernst Ludwig of Hesse. Muthesius, in particular, established the precursor of the Bauhaus workshop training in the German art schools but on a less integrated basis. Important men in the crafts such as the potter and sculptor Gerhard Marcks looked forward to the day "when the workshop would become the art school".

In line with this thinking, Meyerowitz decided at Achimota that the crafts should be taken out of the art school environment. He saw the crafts functioning as industrial craft production units under the aegis of the college. It was sound enough reasoning, except that it was contemplated on too grand a scale. It is unlikely that the pottery section would have developed into more than a healthy workshop, supplying tableware, if there had been no war.

Meyerowitz read the climate well and put forward proposals for a ceramic industry that would supply the *whole* of West Africa with its tableware, tiles, pipes, and insulators. They would also be able to supply the British army, which was in occupation of the Gold Coast. The green light was given for Alajo Pottery.

But for Cardew waiting in London for his sailing orders, Alajo seemed to be the answer to all his ambitions. Not only could he continue to make pots, but he could design for industrial production as well. Stoke-on-Trent had turned him down flat. A short experiment with a Scottish firm proved fruitless. He turned to the Royal College of Art for advice and encouragement, but the head of the ceramic department, William Staite Murray, warned him against his industrial ambitions. "You can't make love by proxy," he said.

In his brushes with the arrogance and pecuniary single-mindedness of Stoke-on-Trent, Cardew had come to believe that the only way in which he could contribute was to grow gradually from workshop to a small factory. Achimota and the Alajo project magically provided the capital and the resources to realize this dream.

But as is invariably the nature of dreams, it contrasted somewhat with the reality. The factory had only two years in which to become productive. During this short time Cardew had to employ and train about seventy people. Although his predecessors, Keith Murray and Harry Davis (both protégés of Leach), had carried out some of the groundwork in the glaze chemistry, fundamental issues such as a regular supply of clay had not been resolved.

There was no machinery, a condition that continued until a year after Cardew's arrival, despite the brandishing of a huge order for the army and trading in the war-time colonial currency of priorities. In everything the project had a quixotic quality. The final touch was the appointment of Cardew.

Cardew was greeted by the heat of Africa at the busy, occupied port of Accra—a different man in some ways from the one who had sought his own path during the twenties. He now had a great optimism about the ability to blend craft and industry. This was a far cry from his days with Leach, when he had had long arguments with Gordon Russell (later to become director of the Council of Industrial Design) at Russell's Broadway workshops in the Cottswolds. Russell wanted to move the crafts in the direction of mechanization, where good design and the machine would replace instinctive craftsmanship. At the time Cardew had argued that there was no substitute for the individual thrower's sensitivity, skill, and judgement.

But if Cardew had now acquired a sympathetic industrial ideology, he was still without the software. In his own way he was as empirical as Stoke-on-Trent. His technical expertise was intuitive rather than scientific, and his knowledge of industrial techniques was negligible. Many times at Alajo he must have wished that his notepad at Matsu's lectures had been filled with ceramic fact rather than drawings of harvest jugs with their legends of "God speed the plough".

A good indication of his attitudes at the time of his arrival are given in an article entitled "Industry and the Studio Potter" that was published in *Crafts* (the magazine of the Red Rose Guild) in 1942. In this he predicted that the industrial tableware designed after the style of hand-made studio ware would become fashionable, and this is what happened in the 1960s. He wrote that the great Staffordshire industry has based its designs for the greater part on traditional thrown shapes evolved by seventeenth and eighteenth century potters, who worked on a handcraft basis:

> Staffordshire to-day has nothing to take the place of this great impetus which has now spent itself, and cannot apparently be renewed from within the industry. The springs from which it came have been systematically diverted and stopped up. The only source left to-day from which a new inspiration can come is the small band of 'artist' potters.

It is ironical that the tin-glazed prototypes he designed in 1939, then roundly condemned by the industry, closely resemble the studio-pottery inspired ware that is produced today by Arabia, Rosenthal, and Wedgewood, even to the detail of craftily applied "impurities".

In the same article Michael makes it clear that his involvement in industry did not extend to endorsing the views of the Bauhaus craft-industry philosophy. He pointed to a serious weakness in the theory of Walter Gropius that craft training can be given in art schools. He rejected the view that after two or even four years a student was equipped to design for industry, adding with relish, "and it is difficult to resist the temptation of citing as proof the actual designs produced by the students of the Bauhaus".

"A long and thorough apprenticeship to the handicraft of any industry is the only sufficient training for a designer for that industry," he argued and, expressing an aesthetic credo that was to be repeated throughout his career, he continued, " . . . a good design in pottery is the product of a tension or 'dialectic' between the demands of pure utility and those of pure beauty, and only a long experience and continual struggle enables you to achieve a successful fusion of the two."

In 1945 Meyerowitz died, and the Alajo project was closed. Cardew lost both a mentor and close friend, and even today his enthusiastic discussions, always rich in quotations and anecdotes, still return again and again to lessons he learned from Meyerowitz.

His favourite is the story that Meyerowitz remembered from his stern apprenticeship in the German Craft Guilds. His master asked of a piece he had just completed, "Is that the best that you can do?"

"Yes, sir."

After a long pause, "Then why do it?"

Instead of accepting a return passage to England, Cardew took a payment in lieu and moved to Vumé Dugamé on the Volta River, seventy miles from Accra and twenty miles from the sea. It was a largish village that had long been a traditional centre for pot making. This folk industry was its primary source of support, and the low-fired earthenware pots were transported up the river and sold to neighbouring communities.

Cardew moved there primarily to make pots. He had made the transition to stoneware at Achimota and was eager to develop further. But he did take three of his hardest working students from Alajo with him, intending to continue the Meyerowitz ideal but on a different time scale and with more human proportions.

There he built his pottery largely from local raw materials, living a precarious existence for three years on an annual budget of £130 by eating the village staples of eggs, coconuts, cassava, and palm oil, with the occasional luxury of fish. The diet may have been full of vitamins as he claims, but it did not keep away median otitis, poisoned hands, and his recurring pneumonia.

Civil unrest nearly proved to be the most fatal of the West African maladies. A group of river pirates had lost their boat during a sortie with a launch from one of the trading companies. They encamped at an inn not far from Vumé and began to attack selected political targets. Through some misinterpreted river cabal, Cardew became added to their list. One morning he returned to his hut after having slept in the pottery shed to find that the mosquito net and bed clothes had been hacked to ribbons by the marauders. From that night on, the chief of the village had pickets placed around the studio until the gang left the territory.

"I think it was done out of a sense of responsibility," Cardew now believes. "I doubt that they particularly valued my presence in the village. Certainly they could never understand what this mad white man was doing and showed no interest in the new technology. But so long as I was resident in the village, the chief felt a duty towards me. I don't think he relished the possibility of the authorities coming from up the river to establish why he had let me get hacked to death in my bed."

The traditional potters of Vumé found no attraction in the new technology that had arrived so suddenly in their village. Perhaps having witnessed the difficulty Cardew was experiencing in making pots, they decided that it was far wiser to remain on their side of the stone age. The women made pots as they had for centuries. The pot is begun in the middle, laying a thick coil of clay on the ground and then building and pulling upwards as she moves backwards around the pot. The shoulder is formed and then, when the mouth is the right size, a neck is built on at a sharp angle to the curve of the shoulder. The half pot is left to harden. Later it is turned over, and the bottom of the pot is commenced by paring the inside rim down to a fine edge with a scraper and then continuing the coil building until a tiny hole is left, which the potter closes with a deft twisting movement.

Then the pot is beaten with a concave wooden tool. The inside is scraped to reduce weight, and finally it is decorated with incised lines on the shoulder and a band of red ochre. By comparison, Cardew's pottery—with its paraphernalia of wheels, kilns, and glazes compounded from clay and oyster shells—must have seemed to the Vumé women like a very long way to get home.

It was at Vumé that Cardew produced some of the most exceptional pottery of his career. He had been moving in the direction of stoneware for some time before his arrival in Africa. In the later years at Winchcombe, the black-and-white ware was really an attempt to achieve a stoneware quality in earthenware.

The output at Vumé was regrettably small, but examples that have survived have been praised by Wingfield Digby as being "amongst the most beautiful modern stoneware ever produced". Certainly the work is distinctive for the almost decadent richness of the Vumé celadon. It fired to a satin olive green, flashing to an unusual vibrant rust colour. Where the bowls and pots had been decorated with the stylized motif of the Vumé lily, the oxide brought up a pleasant metallic, lustrous quality.

In 1948 he left Kofi Attey in charge of the pottery and returned to England, arriving "looking more dead than alive" as Pleydell-Bouverie recalls. It was a reluctant defeat, but Michael's health had become so poor that it would have been fatal to have remained any longer.

Cardew at Alajo Pottery near Achimota. A still from the film
Pottery in the Gold Coast, *1944.*

Washed clay being loaded from the settling pan, Alajo Pottery.
Another still from Pottery in the Gold Coast.

David Cobblah throwing water coolers, Achimota, 1942.

Kofi Attey watching traditional Vumé pottery being transported up the Volta River, 1948.

Two views of the Vumé kiln.

An exhibition of the work in Vumé was held in the winter of 1948-49 at the home of Philip Cardew in Regents Park terrace, London. Muriel Rose wisely arrived before the exhibition was formally opened and acquired the best pieces for the British Council, much to the dismay of the Victoria and Albert Museum.

Cardew had to wait until 1949 until he again had access to the pottery at Wenford Bridge. Mariel had rented it in his absence to an Irish family of potters. When they left, Cardew was joined by the Australian potter Ivan McMeekin, and a downdraught first kiln chamber was built.

For a short time, culminating in his Berkley Gallery exhibition in 1950, he made distinctive but uncharacteristic blue, off-white, and buff stoneware. This work continued the new sense of refinement and finish that had surfaced in Vumé. The even quality of the glaze reflected his newly acquired fascination with and respect for the science of the potter.

The catalogue for the exhibition included a comment on clay and design, in which can be seen the firming up of themes that Cardew has adhered to and propagated ever since. "A good potter," he wrote, "loves his clay disinterestedly for its own character, not because it is an obedient mirror for his personal ideals, however interesting they may be."

The article continued with a statement about the times and the sterile esoteric influence of misunderstood functionalism. "Someone has defined vulgarity in art as the means of expression outrunning the content to be expressed—technique outrunning inspiration. It seems to me that this produces not vulgarity but something worse, the ghastly good taste which is a characteristic product of our education."

Cardew was restless in Britain, and it showed in the detached and deliberate output of stoneware at Wenford Bridge. Even though he had suffered so badly at the hands of the African climate, he longed to return and was despairing of ever being able to do so when the post of Pottery Officer for the Nigerian government was advertised. "I was fifty when I went to Nigeria," he says, "and that was when life really began."

ABUJA

When you are doing your work, you and your work are two different things. But when you become the work itself, and do the work, or in other words when the work is itself doing the work, true work becomes possible.

— Sōetsu Yanagi
The Unknown Craftsman

SOME of the thinking of Achimota College had drifted across to the Nigerian government, and in the search for a means of establishing local industry they hit upon the idea of "upgrading" the traditional African pottery to the level of the European peasant potter. It was with that objective in view that they appointed Cardew as the Pottery Officer of the Department of Commerce and Industry. He arrived to find that the colonial epoch had not yet faded, and this task was to be approached in some style without the wartime urgency of the Gold Coast.

Several months of Cardew's memorable first year in Nigeria was spent travelling throughout the country in a government vehicle to acquaint himself with the pottery activity that still flourished. Africa is the last continent on which "archaic" pottery is still extensively practised. The term archaic refers to the total lack of technical development, methods that have not altered since the stone age, as compared to the Chinese evolution through to high-fired porcelain.

Cardew found this folk art to be thriving, limited only by the availability of clay. He had, of course, been aware of African pots from the first day he arrived in Africa. But his interest had been an aesthetic one only. Preoccupied with the enormity of the Achimota project, he had dismissed them as "technically irrelevant".

His interest in the deceptively simple science of the traditional potter quickly developed. During his months of travels into the remotest parts of Nigeria, he was able to indulge this curiosity. He soon realized that there was nothing that could be done to improve the technical qualities of the pots. They were fully effective in the uses to which they were put, cooking food on open fires and storing water. In fact, their thermal shock level was equal and sometimes better than that of stoneware, although the firing (using a fuel of grass, brush, and bamboo) rarely lasted more than two hours. The effectiveness of this short firing was due in part to timing and to the pre-heating of the pots. In the actual firing, the pots were not heated high enough to develop a glass phase (about 720° C.), when the fluxes begin to form a liquid with the free silica in the clay; the fired strength of the pottery was due to sintering alone, without the help of any liquid or glass.

As the trip continued, as often on foot or horseback as by vehicle, the complexity of the traditional craft began to show itself. Decoration that Cardew had thought to be merely ornamentation was invariably for a practical purpose, such as to increase the strength of the pot in the case of ribbed decoration and to decrease porosity when given a burnished finish or when painted with Makuba lacquer (an extract from the African locust pod).

Forming techniques varied slightly from region to region. The most primitive method used is to place the prepared clay on a shallow calabash and to beat out a hollow in the centre using the hand. The potter then moves backwards around the pot and with a rhythmic motion pulls up the wall of the pot until it is betweeen half and a third of its size. From then on coils of clay are added to the inside of the wall, and the potter continues to move rapidly backwards during the coiling. The shoulder and neck are built up from coils attached to the outside of the pot walls.

The Nupé potters have developed this. They use two calabashes as a sort of primitive wheel, rotating the pot with the potter seated. Once the pot is half complete, coils are added, and the pot is finished in the usual manner. In Yoruba country there is a tendency for potters to concentrate in a few large centres. Here a technique close to press moulding is applied. Using an old inverted pot as the mould, a slab of clay is beaten over the shape with a wooden paddle. It is then consolidated by rolling a corn cob over the surface. Finally it is finished by hand. The pot is left to harden, and the next day coils are added.

Most of the craft laws are laid down by the environment. In the far North, for instance, where water is extremely scarce, Cardew found that the pot-making technique accommodated this. Balls of clay were rolled in wood ash. These were placed in a saucer-shaped depression in the floor and beaten. When the elipsoid shape of their traditional water flask was nearly complete and it became difficult to use the dumbbell-shaped beater, a stick with a knob at the end was inserted into the piece and the pot finished off. Unlike the techniques of other areas, no water was required up to that point of the process. It was only when the neck was joined to the body that a small amount of water was used.

His travels took him to Abuja, where at the emir's home he saw a magnificent collection of pottery. "There were great storage jars, water pots, casseroles, bowls, flasks, and big jugs all decorated with incised designs, partly geometric and partly in a stylized or schematized kind of naturalism: scorpions, lizards, crocodiles, chameleons, snakes, birds, and fish. The whole design was enriched with delicate impressed patterns obtained by rolling small pieces of homemade string or notched wood over the surface of the clay, sometimes as horizontal banding and sometimes in vertical panels." On being asked who made these pots, the emir said that it was a woman of Kwali named Ladi. She was later to play an important role in the acceptance of the pottery centre.

On his return to Lagos, Cardew was faced with the very delicate task of informing the officials that the only thing that could be done to traditional pottery was "to leave it alone". Yet at the same time he wished to retain his position and remain in Africa. In this memorandum Cardew pointed out that there were certain areas in which skilled potters (the Ibos, for instance) were producing imitations of European porcelain in their soft ware. In these places scattered about the country, there was a new life-style emerging that could make use of glazed ware, and the setting up of a few carefully selected pottery training centres could provide the craftsmen to cater for this need.

The report he presented, "A Preliminary Study of Pottery in West Africa," in June, 1950, drew very careful distinctions between what should and should not be done. But in phrases such as "leaving aside irrelevancies such as the so-called art ware, studio pottery and so on . . . " he began to express his growing dissatisfaction with the validity of modern studio pottery.

For Cardew the report represented an important process of assembling his attitudes to pottery, or as he puts it, "establishing his sanity", referring to Compton Mackenzie's *Sinister Street*. In this, an old lady gives her nephew the advice, "In your first two years you must establish your sanity; in the third you may display your charm; in the fourth you can do anything you please". In effect, that represents an accurate summary of Cardew's Nigerian tactics, although he accelerated the chronology somewhat.

The report was considered as "an inspired piece of work", and not only did Cardew retain his job, he was even promoted to Senior Pottery Officer. "Be careful," warned the man from textiles. "When they discover you can write a memo that makes sense they will never let their hands off of you."

Cardew had no intention of succumbing to the fate of being a desk-bound bureaucrat. In 1953 he was required to set up the training centre for the North, and by a happy set of circumstances, Abuja was· selected, although it was some seventy miles from the nearest railhead or bank. He left with a cautionary word from the Commerce and Industry Department: "Don't think that you are leaving us Mr. Cardew. You will stay at Abuja until we have appointed three pottery officers and then you will come back here to manage them and the centres."

True to their word, six months after his arrival at Abuja he was summoned back to his desk in Lagos. At this stage Cardew betrayed an instinct for cunning one would not have suspected in so forthright a man. He had taken the precaution of learning the Hausa language, noting that absolutely nothing could be achieved without it in the North.

The resident, a powerful provincial governor, had visited Abuja in its first few months and noted with some satisfaction this enthusiastic man who spoke the local language and had already been able to produce

Pottery Training Centre, Abuja, Nigeria, 1962.

Preparing the clay.

Decorating the coiled pots.

Pre-heating.

Packed for firing.

Firing the pots.

The finished product.

A throwing lesson with Cardew watched by Kano and Gugong Bong, Abuja, 1959.

Kofi Attey and Cardew with the cover to the underground clay store, Abuja, 1962. Clay could only be made once a year.

Buying Abuci clay from Gwari women, Abuja, 1959.

Water or beer pot from Gwazunu, N. Nigeria, 19th century. H. 45 cm.

Water or beer pot from Yewuni, N. Nigeria. H. 43 cm.

Ladi Kwali demonstrating traditional pot coiling at the Royal College of Art, London, 1962.

Clement Kofi Attey at Abuja, 1961.

Bawa Ushafa making handles at Abuja, 1965.

Cardew and Seamus O'Brien, Cardew's successor at Abuja, building the kiln at Jos.

Abuja Pottery Centre, 1962.

the first trial firings of glazed pottery. Not only did he like Cardew personally, but he enjoyed his Hausa accent! When Cardew was asked to return, the resident was enraged and, using all the influence of his position, telephoned Lagos and stated simply and emphatically that "Cardew stays where he is".

"If it were not for the blacks," Cardew likes to quote Nigeria's first prime minister, Ababaker Tafewa, "I'm sure that the whites of the South and the whites of the North would have had civil war a long time ago."

The area is the only emirate that was not defeated in the Holy Wars and so has a unique place in the country's Muslim history. Abuja is a small Hausa town in the centre of Nigeria and not the ideal siting for a pottery. At Abuja the potters were women and so could not become involved in the centre. The Nigerian woman has an arduous life. Pots are made in between gathering all the firewood, cooking, running the household, producing and bringing up children, and assisting on the farms. She was unable to interrupt this "career" for a four-year course at the centre. The potters came from the north of Zaria, where pottery is a male tradition.

The construction of the centre began with Cardew choosing a spot "where the bare hills rise in steep monolithic domes out of a grassy plain and bounded by a small perennial river, which at the pottery falls in a series of broad cascades over a granite shelf".

Cardew remained at Abuja for fourteen years, creating an establishment that drew 100 percent of its requirements from the local environment. This required the talent of a geologist as much as that of a potter. The clay was brought in by African women from some miles away and bought for a few pence per pot at noisy morning markets.

The clay was not suitable in its natural form and had to be blended. Refractory clay for the kiln furniture and bricks came from kaolin of the Jos Plateau, two hundred miles away. The glazes used at Abuja were of a "porcelain type" and compounded from pure quartz sand, felspar, and limestone with a little fluorspar and clay. Felspar is abundant in the Abuja area, with the best quality coming from the nearby columbite mines. Iron oxide was obtained by placing scrap iron in the kiln during firing and rendering it to flakes.

To obtain suitably pure limestone required an expedition to Kabba Province. There they would camp out and employ carriers to transport it to the nearest road, seventeen miles away. By sheer luck Cardew later found a suitable source more conveniently situated between Abuja and Minna. Fluorspar was only available from the Afo Hills in Benue Province, where they collected enough waste fluorspar at an abandoned mine to last several years.

At Cardew's request the emir sent for Ladi Kwali before the pottery had been built. Mariel was there on one of her visits to Africa, and the two women, bound by the universitality of feminine interests, got along splendidly. Ladi was prepared to work there and then, but was rather perplexed when told to come back again *sai wate biyu*, "in about two months", which by Nigerian standards meant an eternity. Ladi could not understand the need for a kiln or pottery, since her pot-making had always been done in the open, and she left rather sadly, promising to return.

When Cardew was ready to begin, she was nowhere to be found, but eventually was traced to Minna, where she was running a shop. It took two years for her to arrive, and at first it did not seem likely that she would stay. The wheels, kilns, and processes were foreign to her, and the pottery was an all-male establishment.

After observing for some time, she announced that she wanted to work on the "machine", as she termed the wheel. She took to it very quickly, which did not surprise Cardew, since she already possessed two of the main skills required by a thrower, a mature sense of form and an intimate knowledge of clay.

At first she refused to decorate her wheel-thrown work. The stone age and the mechanical age cannot be crossed in a single step. But gradually she took to sgraffito, scratching her sensitive designs through a black slip. At this stage Cardew decided to take the controversial step of glazing and firing her hand-coiled, traditional pots. It was one of the few times that Cardew had encouraged the creation of a purely art object, for once the pots had been made in stoneware, they were too heavy and too expensive for their basic function of carrying water.

This seems to be a contradiction of the "hands off" policy that Cardew emphatically advocated earlier. But Ladi Kwali was an exception. She was a potter who had already walked across from her "archaic" tradition. "I've always argued," says Cardew, "as my master Meyerowitz used to argue, that one must not worry, because these are still the same people. Whatever it is in their work that you like will surface again." But that is true only within limits. The pieces Ladi threw were not copies of Kwali pots, yet the quill-scratched designs made on them were undeniably Kwali in character.

"One's problem is that of a gardener. For weeds do spring up. I remember Bawa Ushafa doing a hare design on a plate that was delightfully naive. A visitor to the studio was thrilled with this and was urging Bawa to produce leopards, elephants, and lions. Soon Bawa would be producing what the French so wonderfully term *faux naif*, the phony naive. These are the things one must guard aagainst, the forced development. Also we had the problem that after successful exhibitions we would receive memos saying how marvellous it was that the exhibition had been a success and now 'couldn't we produce pieces that were *really* attractive for sale at the airports'. The only defence one has against this is the cussedness of the individual."

Yet Cardew found himself constantly having to defend Abuja and what he was doing there. One woman who ran a crafts shop in London travelled all the way to Abuja because she had heard of this pottery in the middle of the West African plains. She was appalled when she saw the work and remarked that she had not travelled a few thousand miles to see pots that could have been made at the Leach Pottery in St. Ives.

"I don't suppose she realized it," said Cardew, "but she was really paying me a great compliment. Not that the work was anything like Leach pottery, in fact. But that we had come so far with our technology to rate a comparison was really very flattering."

Many years later, in 1971, Cardew spoke to a crafts workshop audience at Arrowmont School in Gatlinburg, Tennessee about the difficulties and opposition he had experienced in Africa. "Many people said to me, particularly the more doctrinaire type of anthropologist, "You are doing a very wrong thing, Mr. Cardew. You are imposing these disgusting Bernard Leach type beer mugs or tea bowls on these innocent Nigerians." The problem, however, pointed out Cardew, was one of new life-style. Even though the Nigerians have a long and splendid pottery tradition, it has never before encompassed tea drinking, which was becoming popular in Nigeria.

"So they have to learn by example in the same way as we did in the seventeenth century. One day they will be able to translate their pottery forms into a teapot. But it cannot be forced. As William Blake said, 'We who dwell upon earth can do nothing for ourselves, everything is conducted by spirits, the same as digestion or sleep.' I am very fond of that because it sums it all up."

In 1958 Cardew used his summer leave to arrange and hold an exhibition of his and his students' work at the Berkley Gallery in London. The exhibition was a sell-out and attracted considerable attention in the British press as well as extensive coverage in the *West Africa*, a magazine published by the *Daily Mirror*. Ladi Kwali's pots, in particular, had created a minor sensation and sold for the "unbelieveably high price of about £12 each".

On his return to Nigeria, Cardew expected censure for his personal entrepreneurship. Apart from a slightly loaded "we hear you had a profitable holiday", the reaction was quite the opposite, and basking in the glory of cuttings from *The Times* and other publications, Cardew managed to silence the baying of Abuja's financial critics. The Nigerian government repeated this example in 1962, holding exhibitions in Paris and London that were opened by the emir of Abuja. Cardew and Ladi accompanied the exhibitions and gave demonstrations in Britain. This was followed by an invitation from Philip Rosenthal to demonstrate in Germany, which developed into a triumphant tour of the European capitals.

Ladi's success had the effect of attracting more women to Abuja, and the traditional style of decoration flowed from the women to the men. The influence also showed in Cardew's work, although the decorations on his bowls and later his large stools were not that far removed from the simple decorations at Winchcombe. The major difference was that the motifs now became increasingly rectilinear. His casserole shape changed to that of the Gwari traditional casserole. Overall, there was a greater directness, even harshness, in the work, but looking beyond the superficial, it was still the same man.

The success that Abuja began to enjoy did not spread. The policy of putting potters through a four-year course to set up their own potteries was one of the necessary fallacies that kept support flowing to Abuja. One of the only successful potteries was that set up by Cardew, Kofi Attey, and Jos Museum. The museum had a site for a pottery and had long entertained the idea. The limitation was a lack of funds, and this the museum had once explained to a visiting American lady from Massachusetts. In 1963, some ten years after the visit, the sum of £1,400 arrived as a bequest to start the pottery. Cardew received a telegramme from Bernard Fagg reading, "Fairy Godmother sends money for pottery". He immediately closed Vumé and brought his close friend, Kofi, to run the pottery.

In 1965, after fourteen years of defying the African climate, and the bilharzia infested Iku River (in which he continued to bathe even after his unpleasant cure from that disease in 1959 at the London Hospital for Tropical Diseases), Cardew returned to the "Island of Britain" and Wenford Bridge to begin his working retirement, as the frenetic years since his return have been termed.

Of course there could be no other type of retirement for a man like Cardew because he does not accept any Western dualism of life and work. Life to him *is* work. To Cardew the most satisfying word on this subject is that by Sōetsu Yanagi, the Japanese philosopher:

> When you are doing your work, you and your work are two different things. But when you become the work itself, and do the work, or in other words when the work is itself doing the work, true work becomes possible.

WENFORD AND BEYOND

Tell me Mr. Cardew, do you also make pots?

— a lady from the audience

SOON after his return to Wenford Bridge, Cardew was joined by Hym Rabinowitz from South Africa and a succession of friends and students. His output since 1966 has suffered in quantity because of his extensive travelling and writing. But aesthetically it was a junction point for many of the influences he had felt and appreciated in his previous forty-five years of potting. He began to produce stemmed coffee bowls that derived from 800 B.C. Cyprus (see Pl. 36, *Pioneer Pottery*), pottery stools inspired by the wooden stools of Nigeria, and rose bowls echoing his stoneware of 1949-50 and the slipware of Winchcombe.

Cardew's strong affection for earthenware is one of the distinguishing features of his work in the latter years, as can be seen in his superb translation into stoneware—in the green platters with combed design and, more directly, in the striped and dotted decoration of his gold and brown rose bowls. "By temperament I am still an earthenware man," Cardew maintains. "I miss the crispness of that body and those strong, clear, bright colours. My only dissatisfaction with earthenware and the reason for my move was on technical grounds. When I discovered that my belief that one could make earthenware better by firing it higher was incorrect, I turned to stoneware."

Cardew speaks with fondness of many of his pupils and potters who have worked with him from time to time, but his affection is less restrained when he speaks of Svend Beyer, who joined him in 1969 direct from Exeter University. "Affection," countered Cardew, "No, I speak of him with awe and fear. He is more than just a potter, he is a force of nature. Everything comes to him so easily. Now one could say 'ah this kind of facility must be dangerous to his talent'. Then you can say the same about the infant Mozart. I'm not saying that Svend is Mozart. What I do say is that he is easily my best pupil and I believe that his extreme facility will be very useful to his talent."

Svend exhibited one of the more exciting traditional pieces at the 1972 International Ceramics Exhibition at the Victoria and Albert

Museum. In 1973 he left Britain, spent several months in Korea and then moved to America for a short time, where he set up a workshop and built a climbing kiln of the Korean style.

Writing and travel has occupied much of Cardew's time since his "retirement" from Africa. In 1969 his *Pioneer Pottery* was published. It shows the many facets of this man—geologist, chemist, scientist, philosopher, and, above all, pragmatist. Cardew only began to become seriously involved in the science of pottery at the age of forty. At Achimota he suddenly found himself to be "a man masquerading as a potter, whilst I had no knowledge about pottery whatsoever".

In 1944 he wrote to Beano and spent two weeks in her large Wiltshire home copying "obediently and penitently" the notes that she had taken at the St. Ives fireside lectures. Later in Abuja he began to consider writing a pottery manual for practical as well as political reasons. "A published book had a good deal of prestige in a close community like Nigeria and would certainly get all the teachers on my side." Abuja lived in the constant shadow of the government accountant's axe, and Cardew was ever mindful of the need for allies.

The bones of *Pioneer Pottery* are the eight lectures that he prepared for the "Geology for Potters" course that Henry Hammond organized for Cardew at Wenford Bridge. The thirty or so people who attended the course spent several days travelling about the Cornish countryside in jeeps and trucks to visit granite mines, ball clay pits, and china clay processing plants. The lectures were later painstakingly assembled and reproduced by Hammond, who was assisted by Michael (Seamus) O'Brien.

These were added to and enlarged by Cardew over the next six years, until in 1966 the manuscript was finalized and dispatched to the publishers, who complained that it was too long and "not what we expected, Mr. Cardew". Cardew refused to withdraw a single word, and eventually the book appeared in 1969. By 1974 it was in its third printing.

The reviewer for *Pottery in Australia* summed up the reaction to the book by saying, "*Pioneer Pottery* marks a milestone in the development of artist-potters in the English-speaking community. For some years many potters have felt the need for a book that could act as a sequel to Leach's book, both freeing them from perhaps too great a dependence on Japanese technique and usage, and at the same time enabling them to progress further in the development of pottery that lives and grows out of its own environment. This is such a book."

Arts and Community found it to possess "an individual and original viewpoint with much technical and traditional information that is not found in any other pottery book" and *In Fact*, the journal of the British Ceramic Research Association, called it "perhaps the best book yet available to the potter who intends to go-it-alone".

Just before the book was published Cardew paid his first visit to America. "I had a burning desire to visit that country. Why? I wanted to be stimulated. I was finding the close society of British potters just a little suffocating. And stimulated I was. America is a country that contradicts anything and everything one has heard about it. It is so diverse that it simply defies generalization."

The visit lasted from June to October 1967, and for eight weeks of that time Cardew taught at the summer school of the University of Wisconsin. He then went on to Los Angeles and worked on a film that was never completed with Kent Benson, a friend and fellow potter whom Michael had met when Benson was on a Peace Corps assignment in Nigeria. He returned "an utter physical wreck" and had to postpone his New Zealand visit until mid January of the next year.

Ivan McMeekin, who had worked with him at Wenford in 1949-50, invited Cardew to assist in a scheme financed by the University of New South Wales to teach pottery to the Australian Aborigines. There he spent six months involved in "one of the most fascinating and instructive periods of my life".

He arrived in Darwin in March, after two months in New Zealand, just in time to select the first batch of trainees, who would then work at Darwin, a settlement of about thirty thousand people and the only town of any size in the sparsely inhabited Northern Territory of Australia. The process of selection was very subjective. There was no alternative, since here was the extreme case of a people who were both still "primitive" and had no pottery tradition whatsoever.

It was uphill work both intellectually and physically. Much of the hard labour of the pottery had to be done for the trainees because they did not have any concept of what Cardew terms "the doctrine of the dignity of labour".

"You'd say, come along now Geoffrey, you must do some work. And he'd answer, 'Why should I?' Which is a very good twentieth century question and not easily answered to a people who have a tradition of living on the skill of the hunter and no agrarian background at all."

In order to give them a reference point, Cardew produced his usual work and encouraged them to reproduce it. "In the circumstances, what else could I do. Teaching a child in Britain to write or an Aborigine in Darwin to do pottery is largely the same. You cannot say 'don't do as I do, do it in a way that expresses your personality'. That's nonsense. So the best thing is to say, 'do as I do', and then at least the pupils have something to kick and react against."

The extent to which Cardew was stimulated by this involvement showed in the writings following his return to Wenford Bridge in January, 1969, which produced both his most universal and at the same time introspective articles. In *Pottery Quarterly* (Vol. 41) he wrote:

When you first begin to learn to use the potter's wheel . . . your first efforts are taken up with trying to control it, to contain it, to possess it. At the next stage when you begin to get some control, two things happen concurrently; first you begin to explore what the clay can do, how far you can go with it, where the limits are. And then you try to turn it into something like what's in your mind. What is in

Wenford Bridge Pottery, 1975.

Cardew with Helen Pincombe and Bernard Leach at the Geology for Potters course,
Wenford Bridge, 1959.

Cardew at the drying pans, Wenford Bridge, 1959.

Unpacking a firing at Wenford Bridge.

Cardew throwing at Georgian College, Barrie, Ontario, 1975.

Cardew in Canada, 1972.

your mind is perhaps some pot you have seen and liked, and you think you are trying to reproduce this form; and so you are, but also you are in fact making something of your own. The effort to reproduce what you saw has already involved you in something else . . . something which is both you and not you.

During the effort to imitate or reproduce, you come up against the limitations of your own technical control. You find you can't quite succeed in creating the exact form you had in mind, but you do the best you can with the rudimentary skill that you have so far acquired. You stretch your technical resources to their limits and the result usually is a new realisation, a re-creation (successful or unsuccessful) of the form you saw.

From this he went on to look at the potter who tries to deliberately and intellectually create a new form, saying that having mentally proposed to oneself that what one hopes to produce is a "new" shape, one proceeds by conscious control to make just that.

But even at best, that will only be a projection of your intellectual way of looking at things. Such pots are like shrines dedicated to your own ego; they come from a conscious act of will, not from the compulsions of love. They will be sterile, ego-bound and esoteric instead of being as all true pots are, generous, common and universal.

This, or something like it, is part of the reason that I found it exciting and rewarding to work with the Aborigines. They don't seem to be so obsessed with their own ego as we are, and are not dried up by our anxious intellectual-aesthetic theories . . . . I think they probably intended [their pots] to be like the ones I made; but they were preoccupied by struggling with a new technique, and so the pots turned out to be different, but alive in a new way.

In 1971 he again visited America to teach at the Arrowmont School in Gatlinburg, Tennessee and to lecture at the Smithsonian Institution in Washington. Those who came to the Smithsonian lecture probably expected a potter who would talk about pots. Instead, they were surprised but not disappointed to be faced with a philosopher. It would seem that the "Greats" at Oxford were not wasted. It was a memorable lecture, which enlisted the views of Malraux, Eric Gill, Graham Greene, Emerson, William Blake, Dylan Thomas, and even Voltaire's Dr. Pangloss to support and expand Cardew's own credo.

While in America, Cardew actively campaigned to bring Ladi Kwali there and succeeded in winning over Charles Counts. In 1972 the arrangements were completed, and Cardew, Ladi, and Kofi did a two-and-one-half-month whistlestop tour of America and Canada, doing forty-five official demonstrations and lectures and several others that were not scheduled.

It was thought that the work of Ladi would have particular significance to the blacks in America, who had been cut off for centuries from their African culture. But it was less successful on that level than the professional do-gooder would have hoped. Many blacks were totally indifferent to her work.

Cardew delivered a lecture at each demonstration. On one occasion a woman in his audience approached him afterwards and said, "Tell me Mr. Cardew, do you also make pots?"

In his lecture he took the opportunity of replying to Thelma McCormick of York University, who wrote a paper that substituted what she called "amateur culture" for folk art. To Cardew, whose favourite axiom is one he borrowed from Eric Gill—"an artist is not a special kind of man but every man is a special kind of artist"—this idea was ridiculous.

He retaliated by saying, "Amateur, professional—how I hate those rigid categories. Amateur just means you love it; professional merely means that you are good enough at it to earn your living that way. But a good professional, if he stays alive, will never lose the spark and the freshness, even some of the clumsiness coming from his probably amateur beginnings. And the amateur is always being drawn on irresistibly by glimpses of things that at the beginning he never thought were in his range."

In 1974 Cardew was introduced to a much wider audience by the film *Mud and Water Man*, directed by Alister Hallum and jointly sponsored by the Arts Council of Great Britain and BBC Television. Hallum is a potter turned film-maker who first met Cardew in Darwin and continued on there for some while. His knowledge of the medium resulted in a particularly sensitive film.

For Cardew it was an opportunity to take a nostalgic journey back to the derelict pottery at Vumé and the "new" Abuja. Since his departure in 1966, the mud and thatch huts had been replaced by new and impressive concrete buildings. This did not distress him, much, for he had loved the Gwari village atmosphere of the Abuja he remembered. "Nigeria is a modern state, and this development is what the aspiring potter would now expect to find in a government institution."

Mud and Water Man is Cardew's title. It is an amusing one, but certainly not accurate, for there is much too much fire in Cardew. Seventy years of living life to the brink, hindered only by recurring illness from a body that had "become a surly and reluctant servant", has not cooled his ardour for life. His foot still taps with impatience when the talk or activity loosens the zestful rhythm that is his metre.

Beano says that she imagines that the goblin on his shoulder has always been Edward Lear. "Natural enough, since it was his great-aunt who loved Lear and was loved by him, though they never got around to marrying. The influence shows in many ways: in his always individual attitude to things, his oblique sense of humour, his wanderings about the Great Grombodian Plain. In some of his more personal pot decorations, too—the solemn fish, the slightly sinister owls indicated in two lines on goblets, the ostrich on a plate making a face at a wisp of thistledown.

"And like Lear again, wherever he goes he makes friends; whenever he talks, people laugh. He has written one of the best books on pottery. And he has made pots. His odd and erratic career is littered with them. Steeped in tradition, but tradition always freely used; pots made because the potter wanted to make them; made for use; idiosyncratic, sometimes funny, often splended. No mean achievement one would suppose."

IN PERSPECTIVE

If the writer has used the clay of life to make his book,
he has only used what all men must, what none can keep
from using.

— Thomas Wolfe
Look Homeward Angel

THE process of learning about Cardew is very much like opening a set of Chinese puzzle drawers. Like the drawers, Cardew has a contradictory logic. Small drawers reveal larger drawers, modest facades hide new dimensions. There is an overall and seductive relationship between interior and exterior that misleads those who look only for the obvious.

Those who have found him an elusive and difficult talent to define have tended to label the drawers in Cardew's life: Traditionalist, Leach School, Functionalist, Master Craftsman, and even Great White Craft Missionary. It is important, therefore, to look at some of these to get a clearer perspective of Cardew's complex motivations.

The term traditionalist is one that has been applied to men like Cardew, Leach, and Hamada. They never use it themselves. But since the label exists, it is important to establish its meaning. As a deprecatory term it is used to label artists who draw from the past, as compared to those who think to rely on their own creativity alone and attempt to be totally contemporary.

To me, Cardew seems to be a traditionalist in the purest sense. He acknowledges that the craftsman must, in the words of William Blake, "drive horse and cart over the bones of the dead" if he is to achieve any universal qualities in his work. T. S. Eliot enlarged on this argument when he said that "No poet no artist of any sort has his complete meaning alone. His significance is the appreciation of his relation to the dead poets and artists." This is not the indolence of nineteenth century Romanticism, but a much more basic realization that the past can be the road to the future.

The main division between traditional and contemporary potter is the role of the ego. This is certainly the most volatile element of the craftsman's mix. For the contemporary potter, it overrides all other considerations. He is convinced, as much by mass media as by the art school structure, that he must pursue self-expression. Developments such as minimalism, systemist and conceptual art encourage him to achieve this by the most direct and immediate route. Repetitive work is an anathema; each piece must emerge from his own impulse directly, be creatively flawless, and unique.

Cardew's point of departure from the modern movement is not that he objects to the concept of the "pot as art" so much as he does not believe in the route being followed. The only chance of capturing the creative spirit, he maintains "is by stalking it and taking it by surprise, you have to approach the mystery by an indirect road. That indirect road is skill, or craftsmanship—not only manual control but learning how to overcome all the various obstacles that nature places in the way of art."

The argument against the traditional approach is that by making so large an investment in the craft itself, one suppresses the subjective impulse, the art. Cardew is unconvinced, having found it to be much the opposite in his experience: "the paradox of spontaneity is that it very often springs forth most readily from an arduous discipline. For instance, one can only really be spontaneous and creative in throwing once one has mastered the technique. Otherwise, no matter how casual your approach, you will be too conscious of the process. In all throwing and related processes, the continued and prolonged concentration of repetitive work induces a state of receptivity and of physical and mental polarization in which conscious effort becomes effortless and creative activity gets a chance to begin. The road to a more subjective expression comes from getting on top of your craft, not short-cutting it."

Cardew's wry answer to critics of traditionalism is that "the artist who is an innovator is also the only true traditionalist artist . . . . The others, the practitioners who call themselves traditionalists, are really the traitors of tradition. They murder it in order to be able to take measurements of the corpse."

None of this means that the traditionalist is a selfless craftsman, without ego or egotism. Indeed, Cardew has a particularly well-formed ego. It is, in fact, elemental to his role. His predecessor, the country craftsman, was a humbler man. He was so because he lived in a society both more and less structured than ours. His values and role were circumscribed and defended by his community. Today the *need* for the craftsman's goods has been replaced with a *demand*.

Where the former is purgative and an evolutionary force, demand may be a succubus and easily becomes a materially rewarding kiss of death for the craftsman. For this reason Cardew has always lived by the view that "the world only follows those who have despised as well as served it", always making pots to please himself first. "The most important part of the potter's function is to guide the public, not merely giving it what it wants but revealing to it new things, which will awaken and satisfy new and hitherto unrecognized needs. The potter must lead the public to want what he wants," he says, "then they will come to him because in his workshop the potter's art is alive."

The modern craftsman's commitment to his craft and his conviction about the rightness of his own way and work must be *total* in order to bypass the possibility of becoming a tool of fashion. Seen from the outside, this conviction may seem to be a kind of arrogance. But it is conviction born of experience, of constant self-challenge that nourishes and replenishes the potter in maintaining a standard of craft. This entire question of commitment and confidence relates to the basic reason for becoming a craftsman—the craftsman's original and unending love affair with his materials and techniques. It is this point that contemporary "creative" potters find difficult to appreciate—why and how can a man of Cardew's rambling intellect find outlet in, by their definition, such constrained and physical limits? Cardew's friend Katherine Pleydell-Bouverie sees no contradiction in his double image of repetition-work craftsman and erudite twentieth century philosopher. "It is all understandable," she confides, "if you appreciate that Michael has the creative temperament of a seventeenth century intellectual, part savage and part mystic," a statement that shows rare insight into Cardew's personality. In its way it also explains the ease with which Cardew, with his background of refined Edwardia, was able to make the cultural transition to tribal Africa.

Not all are as understanding. It was certainly in the direction of men like Cardew that Gillian Naylor nodded when referring in *The Arts and Crafts Movement* to "the eccentric fringe with its aura of the homespun and the country dance". In the non-conformity to plastic life patterns, many see an anachronistic rejection of the twentieth century.

But Cardew's intellect will not and cannot be constrained by anything like a cultist pursuit of anachronism. No apology is needed for delight in country dance or bathing in a winter river. Such things do not refute being a well-informed, contributing member of today's world.

If anything, Cardew's traditonalism has sharpened his appreciation of the present and has given him an objectivity that many of us, caught up in the hurly-burly of our time, seem to miss. This is particularly well illustrated in "The Fatal Impact," a lecture he delivered at Washington's Smithsonian Institution. In this he uses the historian's tools to analyze the impact of the present on the future.

His enjoyment of modern art, particularly Andy Warhol and David Hockney, does not extend into his own branch of the arts. Some look upon this as the blind spot of traditionalism, but one could equally argue that it is the result of a very specific set of values. He appreciates the work of only a handful of his contemporaries and then with reservation.

His standards are exacting. His main criteria in judging a pot is form. This, he claims, represents 95 percent of the pot, and no amount or quality of decoration can compensate if this fundamental is unsatisfied. He goes further, teasing his staunch functionalism, "a teapot has little to do with the efficient pouring of tea, it is first and foremost a poem written in form".

Perhaps the best indication of Cardew's views on modern ceramics is contained in a review of the 1972 International Ceramics Exhibition held at the Victoria and Albert Museum in London. Writing for *Ceramic Review*, he said, "I am not attuned to picking up the heavier messages, the *mitteleuropäisch* expressionism, the exercises in ceramic gymnastics and bombastics."

Yet he has never been tempted to set himself up against the modern movement despite attempts by the pottery establishment to arrange confrontations. He freely admits that while the tour de force craft of the new school intrigues him, he does not understand the motives of the work and is therefore too ignorant to stand in judgement.

The same courtesy has not been extended to Cardew. The drawer labelled "Leach School" illustrates his dilemma of having been acknowledged without having been understood. While his work has been included in most major publications and exhibitions on modern pottery since 1928, nearly all have catalogued him as one of the products of the Leach school. Only a few writers, notably George Wingfield Digby and Muriel Rose, have been able to see his St. Ives involvement in perspective and have acknowledged his as a fiercely independent talent.

One can accept that those who apply the label mean to give a compliment by association, but it is totally inaccurate. Above all, it obscures the uniqueness of the man. The label has also clouded the contribution that Winchcombe made to the revival of slipware techniques in England, and, more broadly, Cardew's major contributions to the development of the post-war workshop potter in England and abroad.

It is difficult to think of Cardew as being of the Leach school if one places the pots of Leach and Cardew together. Leach is an artist before he is a potter. This shows in the creative tensions that the pots contain. Cardew is a potter before he is an artist, and so his pots have an altogether different quality. Their beauty derives from the joyous release of life that is within all clay.

Perhaps this can be amplified by examining a quality they share—intuition. Leach, as a sensitive potter, will "go along with the clay" until a point is reached where "eye, head, and heart intercede". This is where Leach's intuitive quality is seen at its best, at the cut-off point between the demands of the clay and the demands of the potter. Cardew's intuition lies in his ability to "go along" with the clay further than any of his contemporaries, except for Hamada, who shares this total sense of communion with the material.

Pottery of the Leach school furthermore tends to have a common characteristic that Cardew does not share. Its desire to bridge the culture of East and West inevitably produces a sense of intellectualism. If there is a counterpointal "ism" in Cardew's work, then, it is assuredly one of athleticism. The contact with clay is direct, physical, and urgent. This shows in his dislike of techniques that in any way lessen this contact.

He has never used wax resist decoration, for instance. He found it too "unsubstantial and shadowy" for pottery, saying that for him it seemed more suitable for textiles. Given the decorative choices in pottery, Cardew has concentrated less on decorative glazes and prefers to scratch designs into the clay itself or to paint with slips.

As a result his work lacks some of the visual sophistication one sees in the work of Leach and Hamada. (He is the only one from St. Ives' early years without a formal education in the visual arts). In its place is naiveté and whimsy, perhaps the most fragile qualities. Such qualities come from the potter himself, his approach to his materials, and his experience— Cardew has retained the essence of the folk potter.

His drawing lessons were learned at the wheel with a slip trailer. All his aesthetic education was subordinate to the needs of the clay. From this evolved a gentle, awkward iconography. What I am saying is not that Cardew is a better potter because he is uneducated in the arts, but rather that he is different. One does, after all, pay a price for knowledge. It opens many doors; it also closes a few, particularly those that give access to direct experience. In this state of ignorance Cardew was able to put his foot in the rapidly closing door of the rural pottery tradition.

Cardew throwing at Cornwall Bridge Pottery, New York, 1975.

Tod Piker and Cardew at wheels, Cornwall Bridge Pottery, 1975.

Pots by Kent Benson, Stanstead, Quebec, 1971 and 1972. H. 24 and 31 cm.

*Stoneware water pot and mug by Ladi Kwali, Wenford Bridge,
1962 and Abuja, 1961. H. of mug 10 cm.*

Coffee pot and four-handled jar by Svend Beyer, Wenford Bridge, 1973. H. 20 and 38 cm.

Stoneware pot by Sias Bosch, White River, South Africa, 1972. H. 60 cm.

Teapot by Seamus O'Brien, Wenford Bridge, 1974, H. 16 cm.

Coffee jar by Seth Cardew, Wenford Bridge, 1974. H. 15 cm.

Cardew looking at pots, Hunter's Lake, Ontario, 1976.

But the key to the difference of, say, a Cardew school and that of Leach lies in another of those labelled drawers—Functionalist. To the Leach school, function is seen as the source of all beauty. To Cardew it is more simply the raison d'être. He has never made decorative ceramics for the collectors. His adherence to functionalism has been total.

It determines all aspects of his work: style, price, and philosophy. His work is in part a reflection of the view of the *Deutsche Werkbund* theorist, Riemerschmidt, that "life and not art determines style". In fact, the word "style" itself seems incongruous. In place of style there is a more esoteric thread called the Cardew signature, which surfaces whether the inspiration is Chinese, Medieval English, or Nigerian folk art.

What emerges has nothing to do with the more cultish functionalism of the jazz age. Cardew's work shows an organic process of change, correction, and improvement. One of the best descriptions can be found in Thomas Hennell's *The Countryman at Work*, where this comment, witten in 1942, appeared in the chapter on Winchcombe.

> Indeed any useful thing calls for alert intelligence in the making forethought and awareness of life's practical needs. It seems that the potter must live in a generous way, for his vessels have this kind of influence in the house. Of [Cardew's] pottery it may be said that nothing comes out which is purely ornament. This kind of unity which should exist in all life's amenities is strangely rare and elusive, it cannot be simulated, it must be through and through.

Function also determines price. Cardew has taken a line between the doctrine of the Natural Price and the Just Price, acknowledging that "art, like roses, is a rich feeder". He plies a middle course, not trying to compete with industrial tableware and yet avoiding individual art pottery for collectors. Even though he has never made for collectors, he has attracted the most intuitive of them, the late Eric Milner-White (the Dean of York), Sydney Greenslade, Henry Bergen, Henry Rothschild, and Bill Ismay.

While Cardew may want his pots to enjoy the natural mortality of utility vessels—to be loved through use, eventually broken and replaced—he acknowledges that society has a way of placing its own value on the craftsman's work. But still he resists this. In his 1975 exhibition at the Craftsmans Potters Association in London his pots were still priced around the £25 mark. Still cheap enough to be used, if with a touch of reverence. Yet, less than a mile away at the Christie auction sale rooms, a 7/6d ($1.00) Winchcombe plate was being sold for £380. "I thought that only happened to you when you died," was Cardew's response. This does expose a modern ambivalence of the workshop-potter. Society has decided on his value, and for the most part his pots are now destined to be frozen on sideboards, in display cases, and museum storehouses.

Cardew the craftsman is probably one of the most intriguing aspects of the man. He has earned the epithet "master" by the only effective gauge, his pedagogic achievements. Students have sought him out from every part of the world. Some like Ray Finch, Kofi Attey, and Svend Beyer learned their craft from him. Yet others like Ivan McMeekin, Hym Rabinowitz, and Seamus O'Brien came under his influence after having been practising potters for some time.

It is not that Cardew invites pupils. On the contrary, he discourages them, putting up a front of formidable indifference. Those who are intrigued by Cardew's infectious humanity and refuse to acccept no for an answer are accepted. And so over the years a Cardew school has evolved. It is loosely knit, sharing a common respect for natural forces and intellectual needs. Throughout the world there are workshops that adhere to Cardew's views: Kofi Attey in Jos, Nigeria; Kent Benson in Canada; Tod Pyker in America; Peter Dicks in England; McMeekin in Australia; and Sias Bosch and Hym Rabinowitz in South Africa. The publication of *Pioneer Pottery* has considerably swelled the numbers.

By and large there is no aesthetic link, but a few potters work in an identifiable Cardew style. One of the most notable is Seamus O'Brien, who has taken the late Wenford forms and given them a strength of a different and very subtle sort. Now there is the promise of a direct second generation: Seth Cardew, Michael's eldest son, has begun apprenticeship at the age of forty, bringing to the wheel a sculptor's sense of form.

Cardew is not comfortable with the drawer marked "master craftsman", feeling that it is inappropriate to a man who has been indifferent to so many of craft's holy cows. Few of his pots can be held up as textbook examples of technical perfection in its decorative art sense. He wants his materials to speak. Usually the finish is summary, even casual. Glazes run or are not uniformly wiped from around the feet. Very often they are over- or underfired. Forms are unconventional; sizes vary.

Cardew is a ware that perfection is a Lorelei that may too easily rob a pot of its life, producing objects that are immaculate yet stillborn. "Perfection is a thing invented by wicked, intellectual man. Nature is absolutely innocent of any such concept." He has never allowed the science of the potter to swamp the humanity of his pots. In this way he is very much like Hamada, who says that "what is unfinished is finished".

The spontaneous quality in his work derives from his temperament as well as from the difficult working environments he has experienced, and sought. There was hardly a time when he was not struggling with limited capital against a difficult kiln, impure and unsuitable raw materials, and different clay bodies in order to establish some sort of order. In many cases, Vumé in particular, the craft achievement in his work is only partially reflected in the pieces themselves. To the casual admirer the pots tell nothing of the unseen craft, the handmade kiln bricks, the treks into the harsh African country to find the raw materials, the improvised equipment and process.

The reason why Cardew has deliberately taken a stand against the soft options in his craft were explained in his article "Amateur and Professional Potters":

So more and more people like to become potters, or at least part-time potters or amateur potters. Most people at first choose to do it the easy way: you buy the clay ready mixed in plastic packets, you get ready-prepared glazes, you buy a prefabricated kiln. Then you have only to learn how to do the *making* part—and goodness knows even then there are plenty of difficulties. But if you remain at that stage, the pots will only be partly yours. Their character is conditioned by that of the clay, the glaze, and the way they are fired. And since all these things—clays, glazes and kilns—are prefabricated and standardized, the pots will be less satisfying than you expected. If they are deprived of half their personality by all these shortcuts, a sensitive potter, feeling that there is something missing, will probably try to replace it by what I call 'a deliberately willed injection of personality'. But it's a mistake, because the something that is missing—call it character or personality or originality or whatever you prefer—is in fact a very mysterious and elusive thing, which cannot be pinned down and captured by direct assault.

If craft is then a means of reaching out for the mystery of creation, it follows that one's craft must be a living—and in Cardew's case—a rugged process. At the same time, the process partakes of the exuberance and involvement of dance. The relationship between the man and his craft is direct, immediate, objective—maker and objects move as partners, separately and in unison, to the same melodies.

The contribution that Michael Cardew has made to twentieth century ceramics is not one of aesthetics. It is more intangible. He has captured some of the life force of the English rural potter and has blended this with other influences to vitalize the "spirit" of the modern workshop potter. It is this life force that his work projects. They are the pots of a man who intends them to be used, enjoyed through use, and quite probably broken, mended, lost, and replaced.

PLATES

Time's wheel runs back or stops; potter and clay endure.

— *Rabbi Ben Ezra*

1. Jug, slipware. St. Ives, ca. 1925. H. 19 cm.
Cornish inscription: MUR MY A'TH GAR NYNTJES EN OL BYS DHE
BAR ("Thou noble pot, I love thee well. In all the world thee hast no equal.")

2. Jar, slipware. Winchcombe, 1938. H. 35 cm.

3. Teapot. Abuja, 1960. H. 19 cm.

4. Bowl. Wenford Bridge, 1975. H. 20 cm.

5. Jug, slipware. Winchcombe, 1933. H. 23 cm.

6. Jar, slipware, ear of wheat motif. Winchcombe, 1933. H. 25 cm.

7. Gwari casserole. Wenford Bridge, 1973. H. 25 cm.

8. Teapot, Vumé lily motif. Vumé Dugamé, 1946–47. H. **28 cm.**

9. Bowl, slipware, fountain motif. Winchcombe, 1937. D. **33 cm**.

10. Jar, Vumé lily motif. Vumé Dugamé, 1946–47. H. 23 cm.

11. Baking dish, slipware. Winchcombe, 1938. W. 29 cm.

12. Handled jar, slipware. Winchcombe, 1930. H. 32 cm.

13. Plate, slipware. Winchcombe, 1929. D. 15 cm.

14. Jug, slipware. Winchcombe, 1938. H. 23 cm.

15. Teapot. Vumé Dugamé, 1946—47. H. 25 cm.

16. Stool, stoneware. Wenford Bridge, 1970. H. 35 cm.

17. Grain jar, stoneware. Abuja, 1961. H. 85 cm.

18. Plate, slipware. Winchcombe, 1936. D. 25 cm.

19. Jug, slipware. Winchcombe, 1934–35. H. 25 cm.

20. Teapot, unglazed stoneware. Wenford Bridge, 1950. H. 34 cm.

21. Rose bowl, line and dot pattern. Wenford Bridge, 1975. D. 30 cm.

22. Handled jar, slipware. Winchcombe, 1935. H. 23 cm.

23. Baking dish, slipware. Winchcombe, 1928. W. 37 cm.

24. Jug, slipware. Winchcombe, 1930, H. 15 cm.

25. Baking dish, slipware. Winchcombe, 1931. W. 36 cm.

26. Mugs, slipware. (l to r) St. Ives, 1924, 1925; Winchcombe, 1926. H. 11 to 16 cm.

27. Jug, salt glaze. St. Ives, 1924–26. H. 17 cm.

28. Lidded jar, slipware. Winchcombe, 1929. H. 20 cm.

29. Lidded jar, slipware. Winchcombe, 1930. H. 21 cm.

30. Cup and saucer, slipware. Winchcombe, 1932. H. 9 cm.

31. Small plate, slipware. Winchcombe, 1933. D. 17 cm.

32. Jam jars, slipware. Winchcombe, 1934. H. 12 cm.

33. Hot water bottle. Winchcombe, 1932. H. 18 cm.

34. Dish, slipware. Winchcombe, 1928. D. 33 cm.

35. Bread crock. Winchcombe, 1936. H. 30 cm.

36. Teapot, slipware. Winchcombe, 1935. H. 37 cm.

37. Large bowl. Winchcombe, 1935. D. 30 cm.

38. Oil (kerosene) lamp. Winchcombe, 1934. H. 20 cm.

39. Cider jar with spigot. Winchcombe, 1935. H. 45 cm.

40. Jug. Winchcombe, 1935. H. 18 cm.

41. Oil (kerosene) lamp. Winchcombe, 1936. H. 15 cm.

42. "DUKE EDWARD forEVER" mug, made to protest the late Duke of Windsor's abdication, slipware. Winchcombe, 1936. H. 13 cm.

43. Lidded jar, slipware. Winchcombe, 1930. H. 17 cm.

44. Casserole. Winchcombe, 1938. D. 23 cm.

45. Teapot. Winchcombe, 1938. H. 35 cm.

46. Sauce boat. Winchcombe, 1935. H. 15 cm.

47. Bowl. Winchcombe, 1934. H. 15 cm.

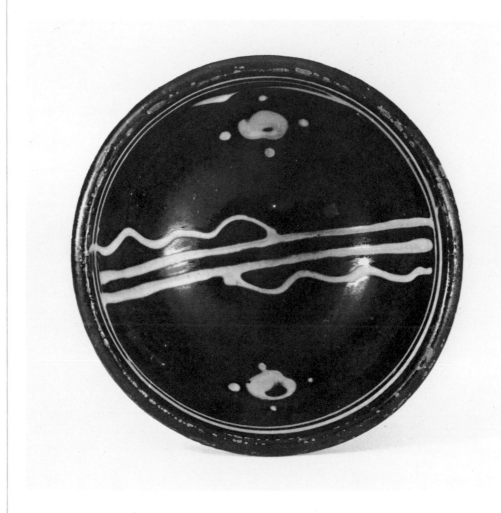

48. Bowl. Winchcombe, 1936. H. 15 cm.

49. Dinner plate. Winchcombe, 1937. D. 25 cm.

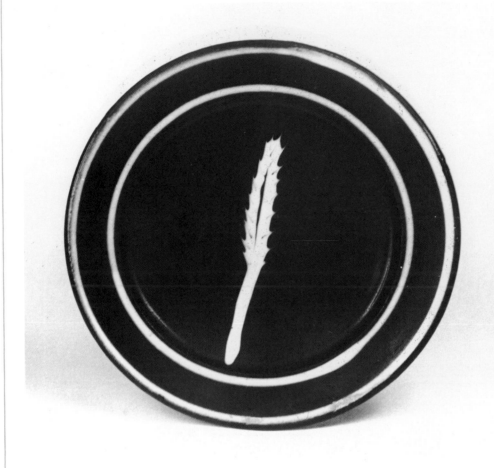

50. Dinner plate. Winchcombe, 1938. D. 25 cm.

51. Cider jar with spigot, fountain motif. Winchcombe, 1937–38. H. 45 cm.

52. Jug. Vumé Dugamé, 1947. H. 13 cm.

53. Plate, stoneware in slipware style. Wenford Bridge, 1958. D. 34 cm.

54. Casserole. Wenford Bridge, 1950. H. 18 cm.

55. Jug. Wenford Bridge, 1950. H. 27 cm.

56. Small handled bowl. Wenford Bridge, 1950. H. 6 cm.

57. Plate. Wenford Bridge, 1950. D. 30 cm.

58. Bowl, decoration derived from Nigerian incised calabash patterns.
Wenford Bridge, 1955. D. 25 cm.

59. Teapot. Abuja, 1965. H. 12 cm.

60. Gwari casserole. Abuja, 1958–59. H. 16 cm.

61, 62. Sauce pots. Abuja, 1958, 1959. H. 8 cm.

63. Small jug. Abuja, 1956. H. 10 cm.   64. Mustard pot. Abuja, 1959. H. 5 cm.

65. Jar. Abuja, 1958. H. 22 cm.

66. Wine jar. Abuja, 1958. H. 95 cm.

67. Sugar caddies. Abuja, 1961. H. 14 and 12 cm.

68. Hot water jugs. Abuja, 1962. H. 14 and 13 cm.

69. Small handled bowl. Wenford Bridge, 1970. H. 9 cm.

70. Gwari casserole. Wenford Bridge, late 1950s. H. 18 cm.

71. Cider jar with stopper. Wenford Bridge, 1966. H. 36 cm.

72. Plates. Abuja, 1959 (left) and Wenford Bridge, 1966. D. 20 cm.

73. Sauce boat. Wenford Bridge, 1969. H. 15 cm.

74. Lidded jar. Wenford Bridge, 1966. H. 22 cm.

75. Cider jar with screw stopper. Wenford Bridge, 1975. H. 25 cm.

76. Dish. Abuja, 1965. L. 45 cm.

77. Colander. Wenford Bridge, 1975. D. 25 cm.

78. Casserole. Wenford Bridge, 1971. D. 25 cm.

79. Stool. Wenford Bridge. 1975. H. 23 cm.

80. Large jar with "stool" lid. Wenford Bridge, 1975. H. 40 cm.

81. Coffee pot. Wenford Bridge, 1974. H. 25 cm.

82. Grain jar. Wenford Bridge, 1976. H. 52 cm.

APPENDIX

Give all thou canst; high
  Heaven rejects the lore
Of nicely-calculated less or more.

— Wordsworth
Ecclesiastical Sonnets

WORKSHOP APPENDIX

This appendix concentrates more on the environment of the workshops than on the actual craft of throwing and making pots. It is devoted to the workshops that were under Cardew's control and so excludes Bernard Leach's St. Ives pottery. However, since Pleydell-Bouverie's eloquent account of the first firing of Matsubayashi's kiln has been quoted here, it is of interest to know something more specific about the St. Ives kiln, which is still in use today, having been converted first to oil then to gas.

The kiln took Matsubayashi nine months to complete, with assistance from Dunn, Cardew, and Pleydell-Bouverie. The failing of the first kiln (which Hamada and Leach built) was its size. It was a small two-chambered climbing kiln attached to what was more a pottery studio than a workshop.

The second Leach Pottery kiln comprised three chambers, each 6 feet high by 4 feet deep. According to Murray Fieldhouse's account (*Pottery Quarterly*, vol. 1, no. 1, pp. 17–27), the kiln had a capacity of 1,000 pieces. Fired with wood (pine logs), it took thirty-five hours to reach 1,250–1,300° C., two-thirds of the time being spent on stoking the first chamber with wood.

The logs measured two feet in length, and two to three pieces were fed into the firemouth every 15 minutes, gradually building up to one-dozen logs every four minutes after the first 2–3 hours.

The first chamber was soaked for 1 hour when the maturing temperature was reached. "By this time," says Fieldhouse, "chamber two had reached 900° C. and chamber three 500° C. from the heat overflow of chamber one." Side stoking then began, the hot air flowing into chamber three if it contained biscuit ware or being diverted up the chimney if it did not.

Another kiln was built in 1925 for slipware. This was a round updraught kiln. The kiln was pre-heated by drip feeding paraffin (kerosene) into a tin of sawdust for two hours. The firing took 12 hours to reach a temperature of 1,050° C. The slipware glaze comprised: litharge 3 parts; red clay 1 part; flint 1 part. The body consisted of 61 parts local red clay from St. Erth, 23 parts water-ground quartz, and 16 parts china clay. Pike's silicious ball clay was used for the white slip, and the black slip comprised: 7 parts red slipware body and $2\frac{1}{2}$ parts red iron.

Part One ~ England

WINCHCOMBE   1926–1939
(Originally Greet Pottery, producing agricultural hardware from ca. 1794 to 1914)

CLAY BODY
Used Fremington clay from north Devon, until permission was obtained to dig clay in the adjoining field. Also experimented with clay from a nearby brickworks, but the kiln would not fire high enough to eliminate severe porosity.

POTTERS
Elijah Comfort was a thrower from Greet Pottery who had been working as an agricultural labourer for twelve years since its closure. He made large wash pans and flowerpots.
Sydney Tustin was employed at the age of fourteen to turn the wheel crank for Comfort. In 1928 Cardew bought a power wheel (driven by a petrol engine) from W. Boulton, Engineers, Stoke-on-Trent. Tustin then learned to throw, and is now an accomplished potter working with Ray Finch at Winchcombe.
Charlie Tustin, Sydney's younger brother joined for a short while in 1932. He made good pots, but was called up during the war and never returned to pottery.

Ray Finch joined in 1936 as an apprentice. Later became a partner and then bought out Cardew's share. In the fifties he made the move to stoneware and today heads one of the most successful workshop potteries in Great Britain.

WHEELS

1. Cardew preferred to use a kick wheel left over from the days of Greet Pottery.
2. A bevel-gear wheel, hand-turned by Tustin for Comfort.
3. Power wheel used by Comfort and later Cardew for big pots.
4. In 1928 Cardew's original 1922 wheel (made in Braunton) arrived from St. Ives, and Comfort began to work on this. He then stopped making flowerpots and washing pans and turned to casseroles, plates, and other tableware.

SLIPS

White ball clay from north Devon provided the white slip. Black slip came from a local clay with iron and manganese oxides.

GLAZES

There were two basic glazes in use at Winchcombe.

galena (PbS)	60 %
local clay	30 %
quartz	10 %

The second glaze substituted white ball clay for local clay. This matured at 1,000° C. (Seger Cone 05 or Orton Cone 07–06).

KILN

The bottle kiln was updraught with four fires. Its capacity was about 600 cubic feet, taking 2,500–3,500 pots. In addition there was a smaller chamber above the dome called a "hovel" used for biscuit firing when required. Ninety percent of the products were single fired (i.e., raw glazed). It was fired with coal to about 900° C., then with faggots (larch, spruce, etc.) to 1,000° C. Firing took 36 hours, and the kiln was fired four times a year. The first firings were very poor. Galena is very sensitive to damp conditions, which cause the lead to volatize and leave the surface starved and rough.

WENFORD BRIDGE   1939–1942

The output from Wenford Bridge was very small due to wartime restrictions. Produced some slipware and experimented with tin-glazed 'earthenware. Used Fremington clay and the same glazes as at Winchcombe. There was no electricity at Wenford, and Cardew used a kick wheel and rope wheel.

Kiln
The kiln was 100 cubic feet, with an upper chamber, or "hovel". It was updraught with three fires and fired as at Winchcombe with coal and then faggots. It was built between 1939 and 1940, single-handed except for a few days' casual help from a visitor.

WENFORD BRIDGE   1949–50 and since 1965

The stoneware workshop at Wenford comprises four parts.
1. Clay stores and grog stores. This contains a vertical pug mill, rope wheel, wedging table, moulds for oblong dishes (3 shapes, 2 sizes).
2. The mill. This contains a crusher-pulverizer; 30 gallon ball mill; 10 gallon ball mill; raw material stores; one all-ball wheel; and a portable whirler.
3. The throwing shop. This area is known in the Wenford patois as "the skittle alley". Contains kick wheel; all-ball wheel; power wheel for big pots; wedging table; clay store.
4. Kiln shed. Downdraught round kiln 6 feet inside diameter (100 cubic feet) and second chamber (updraught) 6 feet diameter with dome and chimney (the old earthenware kiln that was converted by Cardew

and Ivan McMeekin). Also, kick wheel; wedging table; glazes; saggers; and setters (pan-rings).

CLAY BODIES

THROWING BODY: A red body composed of a north Devon (aluminous) ball clay blended with a "fireclay" from St. Agnes (near Hayle), which is about 80 percent very fine sand in a pale clay. To this is added Etruria marl, to give a body colour that will contrast well with white slip and lend itself to combed and sgraffito decoration. A small quantity of mica waste from Stannon China Clay works is added in place of felspar.

north Devon 120 ball clay	*31.9%*
St. Agnes "fireclay"	*37.0%*
Etruria marl	*23.3%*
Stannon mica	*7.8%*

OVENPROOF BODY: This body is porous at 1,270° C. and, like the throwing body, is red and contrasts well with white slip. This is based on the body used for making pressed dishes fired on pan-rings at Abuja:

Sabon gida (plastic clay)	*30%*
china clay	*30%*
sand (30 mesh)	*40%*

and is composed of

north Devon 120 ball clay	*9.9%*
china clay	*29.6%*
Etruria marl	*19.0%*
St. Agnes "fireclay"	*11.5%*
St. Agnes sand	*18.7%*
zircon sand	*11.3%*

GLAZES

STANDARD WENFORD GLAZE: This slip glaze fires black, breaking to brown when applied over both the throwing and the ovenproof bodies. Over white slip it gives amber colours with tints of green and brown extraordinarily similar to galena glazes.

Wenford frit	22.5%
Meldon stone	15.0%
Fremington clay	25.0%
120 ball clay	10.0%
grass ash	10.0%
quartz	17.5%

CHUN GLAZE: This glaze gives translucent grey-blues and grey-greeens and breaks to brown and black where thinly applied over an iron slip. Its character comes from the fused wood ash that Cardew first noticed in the ashpits of the kiln at Vumé, Ghana. Both there and at Abuja this was a white coral-like substance, tinged with pink or pale purple, which made it inviting to grind and use in the glazes. At Wenford a similar material is formed in the ashpits, but it looks black and slaggy and gives less brilliant yet attractive, subdued glazes.

Wenford frit	25.0%
Fremington clay	7.5%
talc	2.5%
quartz	27.5%
Meldon stone	37.5%

ZIRCON GLAZE: A white, nearly opaque slip-glaze opacified with micronized zircon. It is usually applied over a white slip and decoration painted on the glaze with iron and blue pigment.

Meldon stone	21.25%
120 ball clay	30.0%
Vumé frit	26.875%
borocalcite	6.875%
quartz	10.0%
zircon	5.0%

GRANITE GLAZE: Composed of 90 percent finely ground De Lank granite. When iron is painted over it, it gives very sharply defined brushstrokes of rich red-brown of lustrous quality. The contrast between the colour of the pigment and glaze is increased if the glaze is used as a thin wash over zircon glaze. Since the thickness is very critical, slight variations create a background of broken amber and olive greys.

granite	90%
Fremington clay	5%
Wenford frit	5%

MATERIALS

WENFORD & ABUJA FRITS: Fused wood ash from the ashpits of the kilns.

FREMINGTON CLAY: A highly plastic red-firing, fusible glacial clay used traditionally in Devon for glazed and unglazed earthenware.

MELDON STONE: Obtained from a road-stone quarry in Devon. The stone is a fine-grained aplite, which is roasted in the biscuit chamber before being crushed and milled and used in glazes.

GRASS ASH: Mouldy hay carefully burnt by a kind farmer. Washed and used in standard glaze.

STANNON MICA: A secondary mica extracted from china clay during the purification process. It is used in place of felspar in the throwing body.

120 BALL CLAY: Aluminous, very plastic ball clay from near Bideford.

ST. AGNES "FIRECLAY":   This is not a true fireclay, i.e., it is not associated with coal. It could perhaps be described as a pale-firing plastic clay that bounds a pale fine sand; ratio, clay about 15: sand 85. It is barely plastic enough to throw with, used by itself.

Part Two ~ Africa

ALAJO POTTERY   1942–1945

BACKGROUND

When Cardew arrived in September, 1942, some of the pottery activity had already moved out of the Achimota College School of Art. A small, flourishing industry had begun to make porous terracotta water coolers, which had previously been imported from Germany. Thousands of these were being made to satisfy the local demand. They were fired in two large rectangular downdraught kilns (capacity about 200 cubic feet).

Harry Davis, from whom Cardew was taking over, had begun experiments with local materials. He had built (to a design supplied by the Rural Industries Bureau, Britain) a $4\frac{1}{2}$-foot-diameter, round downdraught kiln. He had managed to produce highly successful stoneware glazes using local rock and wood ash. Also experimented with local clays, mostly of a poor quality with unknown and untested physicochemical properties. By blending these with local rock (pegmatite; i.e., felspar) he made an adequate stoneware body. It was ferruginous (i.e., iron saturated), firing dark grey in reduction atmosphere.

In the absence of adequate machines (ball mills), he devised ingenious grinding techniques, breaking up the rocks in an edge runner mill of the type used in crushing apples for cider and then separating the ultrafine fraction by air flotation, employing an improvised exhaust fan. Using the differentials of cars and lorries, he had built efficient hand-turned wheels. Also made slip machines (blungers) with the same improvizational genius.

By September, 1942, the brick and tile plant was more or less operational, although construction was still proceeding. It was set up on a small grant from the Colonial Office of £18,000 and was built near Alajo, a small village in a wide, flat, clay-soil valley midway between Accra and Achimota. Today it is suburb of Accra.

The fuel came from the "Achimota Forest," an artificial but well-managed plantation producing both neem trees and cassia. It provided wood for the kitchens and homes of Achimota College and the pottery and tileworks.

POTTERY PRODUCTION PLANT

This was under construction, using bricks and tiles from the plant and timber from up country. The layout was planned by Davis with prodding from H. V. Meyerowitz, conceptual architect of the entire scheme. In most cases only the shells of the buildings were completed; only two were roofed. The plan envisaged the following:

1. Mill. A large open building (in excess of 100 × 24 feet) with bays for bulk storage of raw and prepared materials. It also housed a $4\frac{1}{2}$-foot-diameter ball mill and a 10-hp. diesel engine to drive it.
2. Open shed. About 60 × 18 feet. Housed the blunger, clay preparation, and settling tanks.
3. Throwing and making shops. About 100 × 18 feet.
4. Store for biscuit-fired ware. Same as above.
5. Kiln shed. This was a vast building, 120 × 24 feet, and designed for four downdraught kilns, each 12 feet inside diameter, 18 feet external diameter. The capacity of each kiln was to be about 1,000 cubic feet, and they were designed to have shared chimneys.
6. Store for finished glazed ware.

A railway was run through all the buildings, bisecting them; the trucks were pushed by hand and used for bringing in clay from the brickwork's clay pit and firewood from the circular saw.

Most of the construction work had still to be undertaken, and apart from three good throwers trained by Davis, Cardew had to train all the staff. The pottery had a firm order of 180,000 pieces annually from the army for everything from dinner plates to egg cups, 200,000 latex cups for the rubber industry in Nigeria, and thousands of low-tension electric insulators and terracotta pots for the Cocoa Research Station at Tafo.

The latter was the only order that Alajo was able to complete during its short life.

Problems were soon encountered. The major one was that the body devised by Davis (67 percent local Alajo clay plus 33 percent felspar [iron free pegmatite]) was not suitable. The main reason was the poor quality of the local clay (see *Pioneer Pottery*, p. 19). Also, the felspar supply was not well organized. It was collected haphazardly from places about thirty miles inland.

Cardew felt that it was impractical to use milled materials in the clay, preferring a natural, vitrifiable clay that would then be mixed with fine sand and some local clay. Such a clay (nearly white) was found at Koforidua, fifty to sixty miles inland. However, it was not available in commercial quantities and could not sustain continuous production.

At its peak the pottery had twelve to fourteen throwers, five men on the blunger and clay preparation, and a team of six on the kiln. In addition, eight throwers working on hand-powered wheels were housed in one of the open sheds making saggers and water coolers. Cardew built a muffle kiln for them and a large artificial dryer for the water coolers. The kiln had eight fires and had to be fired to 1,000° C. because of the poor clay quality. Normally, 900° C. would have been sufficient.

Equipment comprised a diesel engine, edge runner mill, ball mill, blunger, five power-driven potter's wheels, a potter's lathe (which was adapted into a sixth power wheel).

In all, the pottery employed about sixty men plus the builders, masons, bricklayers, and carpenters. Expansion of the pottery continued until its closure, building underground stores for the clay, a canteen, office, etc.

KILNS

Only two of the four planned kilns were built. They were fired several times with water coolers and earthenware to 1,000° C. and then set with glazed ware and fired to 1,250° C. on three occasions.

Refractory Materials

A major drawback was the lack of refractory materials for saggers and bricks. The local clay mixed with sand was only just adequate for use in small kilns. The bricks used in the kiln were high in free silica, so they slagged badly and also spalled (i.e., broke off in flakes). These faults were aggravated in the large kilns. The saggers posed a special problem. In the small kilns, the bungs (pillars of saggers) were only $3\frac{1}{2}$ feet high. In the large kilns they were up to 8 feet. Cardew found out that the refractoriness of refractory materials under load could often be about 300° C. lower than under normal circumstances. Saggers that could easily withstand high temperature on their own collapsed during the second high temperature firing when stacked in heavy bungs.

Hampered by the lack of commercial quantities of clay and refractory materials, the pottery was closed in 1945.

VUMÉ POTTERY   1945–1948

Vumé pottery was begun in October, 1945, with capital of £700. It comprised three potters, Cadew, Clement Kofi Attey, who was a star pupil from Alajo, and Kwami Agbedanu, who learned to throw at Vumé. Equipment comprised a rope wheel (hand turned), a kick wheel of the English type, a hand-turned bevel-gear wheel, which was homemade and did not work well.

The Pottery

This was a long thatch and bamboo shed 100 × 18 feet. The kiln was 6 feet in diameter, round, downdraught with four fire boxes and a capacity of 100 cubic feet. There was also a second chamber, about 4 feet in diameter and 8 feet high; above this the chimney made the construction a total height of 22 feet. There were two underground clay stores, circular and domed ("There is something very religious about domes," contends Cardew). Access was from the top by bamboo ladder.

THE MILL

This comprised a 5-hp. diesel engine with a corn mill for grinding the cassava and maize of the villagers but also used to pulverize grog and rocks. There were also two 15 to 20-gallon ball mills for grinding glaze materials, which Cardew acquired for £10 from a friend in the U.K.

CLAY WASHING TROUGHS AND SUN PANS

Water was pumped to these from the Volta River, but the pump broke down, and the water had to be transported by hand from then on.

CLAY

The Vumé surface clay that the village potters used was tested by Cardew in Alajo in a 2-foot-diameter test kiln. It seemed satisfactory. However, in a bigger kiln with a longer firing schedule, it gave trouble in that it shattered with glaze. Shattering is the opposite of crazing (see p. 72, *Pioneer Pottery*).

REFRACTORY MATERIALS

There were no refractory materials at Vumé. The saggers made of local clay simply melted during high firing. Small quantities of a very silicous refractory earth were obtained from a deep well (60 feet) eight miles away. From Mpraeso Bauxite Mine (another wartime enterprise) a supply of bauxite was obtained. Excellent saggers could then be made from the refractory earth, ground calcined bauxite, and Vumé clay to act as a binder (about 30 percent).

 The standard clay body was less easy to solve. There were plentiful supplies of felspar, 'Pogeddi stone, and Sogankope stone, but there is a mechanical difficulty in mixing a wet ground powder into an already plastic clay body, apart from the theoretical difficulty of accuracy. Cardew made up bodies with kaolin addition (a few cwt had been obtained from Benso in the Western Province) plus soft-fired bauxite (water-ground). Vumé clay and water-ground bauxite alone was too ferruginous. Nonetheless, some of the most successful Vumé pots (teapots, for instance) were made of this. Glaze was made chiefly from local felspar, clay, and oyster shells water-ground to palpable fineness. The usual pigment was natural iron oxide (limonite nodules and laterite).

FUEL

An arrangment was made with the farmers to leave piles of firewood on the riverbanks. Cardew bought a second-hand sea-going canoe and went up the river with this to collect the fuel.

VUMÉ   after 1948

Cardew left Vumé in 1948, handing over the pottery with £30 "working capital" to Clement Kofi Attey. He continued to make glazed ware and water coolers until sometime in 1950. When Cardew visited Kofi on his way to take up appointment in Lagos, he found the pottery in trouble. The kiln wall and the continuous "annular" bag walls were of poor material; they had shifted, leaving too narrow a space for the flames to come up. "Kofi did not have enough experience to realize what was the cause," says Cardew. "His troubles were that the temperature became 'stuck' at 1,000 to 1,050° C. during glaze firing, as it does if a kiln is wrongly designed or if something obstructs the fire's path." Kofi used up all his capital trying to refire, but without being able to produce any articles of commercial value. Cardew was able to spot the cause of the trouble and assist him before leaving. In the end, the pottery was closed down, and Kofi moved to a small pottery at the Jos Museum in Nigeria.

ABUJA   1951–1965

The setting up of the Abuja Pottery Centre began in August, 1951. Alongside the Iku River the first mud and thatch building workshop was fitted (60 × 18 feet). At the one end were six kick wheels, and at the other end was a drying gallery along the lines of the traditional English system.

It comprised posts with one-inch holes at six-inch intervals, which then took the pegs and ware boards.

Before this, a washing plant was built near the Iku River for kaolin with twin settling pits or sun pans and twin weathering-floors (cement rendered) with a six-inch wall surrounding (12 × 12 feet).

A second building parallel to the first was added, and this housed the mill. Then a store and tiny office were added. Then gradually over the next four years a small pottery "village" grew on the site, adding separate round houses for saggers, glazing, biscuit ware, and main kiln (completed in late 1953). The second chamber and chimney stood in the open. Two rectangular buildings (30 × 15 feet) were added; one was a new office, and the other a workshop with five wheels, shelving, and a damp room.

THE KILN

The main chamber was 6 feet in diameter, as at Vumé. But the second chamber was 6 feet with a perforated dome, as at Winchcombe and Wenford, plus a small tapering chamber (hovel) over this. It was built like the test kiln (Nov.-Dec., 1951) from "red earth" bricks dug on site. A few arch bricks made from the so-called Kwali kaolin were used in the most critical parts of the throat arches. The original kiln had none of these bricks. It was used for calcining the Kwali kaolin to make white grog. The lining of the test kiln soon slagged. A new lining was smeared on (plastic kaolin) and was repaired in this way continuously during its three to four years of life, when it was often fired to 1,250–60° C.

The big kiln gave serious trouble after two glaze firings. The dome was built of red bricks that slagged, and the thick slag would fall off. Repairs along the lines of the test kiln were not possible, since the kaolin paste would not adhere to the powdery surface of the bricks. So the dome had to be pulled down and rebuilt with kaolin bricks. By this time a superior quality of kaolin had been discovered.

The throat arches began to give similar trouble, and soon it became apparent that the entire kiln would have to be relined with good kaolin bricks. This was done on a piecemeal basis so that it did not interrupt production for long. "This is the type of running repairs and improvization that one is obliged to use when starting a high-temperature pottery in the bush," notes Cardew.

RAW MATERIALS

At the time of Cardew's first visit to Abuja on tour (November and December, 1950) the emir had assembled some raw materials, including a plastic dark grey clay from Abuci, three miles west of Abuja. Travelling there on horse and foot, Cardew found a flood-plain clay surface in schist country. It was caused by conditions of impeded drainage. The stream had cut a new channel two to three feet lower than the old, leaving the clay in a dry field. Every year, 50–100 Gwari women of Abuci village hacked out calabash loads and carried these (and babies) to the Abuja clay market, where the clay was bought at from 6d to 2/(about 7 to 25 cents) a calabash.

At first the Kwali kaolin from the top of a steep 1,000-feet hill was used. This was unsatisfactory as a long-term source. Eventually two other sources were discovered. The "Majapota" (Major Porter) mine had quantities of true decomposed granite kaolin and extensive exposures of pure kaolin. Later Cardew obtained this from Jos Tin Areas, the company running the mine, by the lorry load at £1 per ton. The cost of haulage from this rugged area on the Jos Plateau (a distance of 250 miles) worked out at seven times that of the raw materials.

The second source was the white clay of Dangara, sixty miles south of Abuja. This was chiefly used to make up 40 percent of a new body. Previously Cardew had made experimental bodies from Abuci clay, but it crazed and made the ware too brittle. The iron content was too high (7.7 percent), and at high temperature the body was also vesicular and sometimes even bloated. Dangara clay, on the other hand, was no use alone because it was not plastic enough (see *Pioneer Pottery*, pp. 33, 74, 75).

A special clay was also made, which was called "white body", although it was far from white. But the iron content was low (at 2.5 percent). This was composed of Sabon Gida clay from the mine of the same name, about twenty miles south of Jos. This was an open-cast mine whose shape was constantly changing because it was worked at one end and back filled as the work progressed. The area must have been an "old" temporary lake dating from the Newer Basalt lava flow period (1–5 million years); the basalt formed a dam, behind which the tin ore accumulated and, over this, the clay. At places the clay was very plastic and practically white, but mostly it was a pale to dark grey with a low iron oxide content in the region of 4.6 percent. The "white body" comprised equal parts of Sabon Gida clay, Dangara clay, and felspar, ball milled and stiffened in pots.

Felspar came from two main sources. The first was a very pure albite (soda felspar) from the Takwashara Tin Mine, forty miles east of Abuja, where the albite was thrown out as a waste product and was collected in bags from the spoil heaps. The second source was of potassium felspar from a turtleback exposure near the Bwari tin workings (about fifteen miles from Abuja). Cardew supervised the use of crowbars, sledge hammers, and cold chisels to continue the "exfoliation" that nature had already commenced. The felspar was used in all glazes (about 60 percent), in white slip (50 percent), and in the special body (up to 30 percent).

Limestone required an expedition to Jakura near Lokoja, travelling the first one hundred miles to Koton Karafi. Arrangements had been made to be collected by the ferry launch and to be taken sixteen miles upstream to Lokaja on the Niger. From there it was twenty miles by vehicle to a 1,200-foot plateau, where the rest house was, after which it was a sixteen-mile trek through the bush to Falconer's Marble (see W. D. Falconer, *Geology and Geography of N. Nigeria*). It was a superb marble, 99 percent $CaCO_3$ with a little graphite. Cardew camped there for five days, remembering it as an impressive place with massive pillars of black rock that were pure white inside. On the trip they obtained eighteen cwt, which was enough for several years.

By chance Cardew discovered a more accessible source of limestone at Kwakuti on the road to Minna with a high content of $MgCO_3$ and some graphite. He enjoyed a measure of fame in Nigeria for this bit of geological detective work.

Other raw material sources included: Ikka talc schist (near Abuci) for a talc body for casseroles; topaz from Jos Plateau for a superior millite grog; zircon (also from the Jos Plateau) was used for small kiln furniture (chairs and saggers; see *Pioneer Pottery*, Chapter 9).

Sand came from Ashera near Dangara, fifty miles south, in granite and gneiss country.

STAFF

Abuja in the sixties before Cardew left consisted of nine throwers (five men and four women)—Bawa Ushafa, Tanko, Peter Gboko, Ibrahim Muhtari, Abu Karo, Ladi Kwali, Isibi Ido, Lami Toto, and Kande Ushafa. The kiln team was headed by Danjuma, with Husani, Gwari, and Naanabi, who were supported at firings by the male throwers.

The English type of kick wheel was used. There were nine of these, of which three were geared to about three to one.

THE FATAL IMPACT

The "fatal impact" (the phrase is not mine, but comes from Alan Moorhead's book of that title) means the effect on all the other races in the world of their contact with Western Man, that expansive, acquisitive, affluent, long-nosed predatory animal who is us. Given the same opportunities, no doubt any other race would have qualified for the same string of epithets (except perhaps "long-nosed"). But the question remains, who provided the opportunities?

The consequences of the fatal impact were summed up in 1836 by Charles Darwin: "Wherever the European has trod, death seems to pursue the aboriginal. We may look to the wide extent of the Americas, Polynesia, the Cape of Good Hope and Australia, and we find the same result." But potters and other craftsmen are only concerned with one aspect of this impact—the death (or rather the "fate worse than death") which usually overtakes the arts of those peoples.

Those arts were the major expression of their culture. Even in the darkest days of the nineteenth century, the more perceptive travellers and observers were impressed by them; not only by the technical efficiency of primitive tools and utensils but also by the loving care with which they were made and decorated, and by the contrast between the supposed abject poverty of the natives and the long hours they willingly spent doing work which seemed to the nineteenth century observer to have no significant effect on the "economic value" of the works produced.

Their "artifacts", as we quaintly call them, are basically sacred, and they had to be given all that devoted care in order to confer power and significance on them. To the people who made them it would be unthinkable to treat them as mere utilities lacking this inner meaning; and the point I want to make is this: there is only one species of person in our modern societies in the affluent West whose attitude to their work is comparable, and that is the species called Artists. Artists or Craftsmen would thus seem to be specially well qualified to make some contribution towards mitigating the effects which Western contacts have on these arts;

but they very rarely get any opportunity to do anything about it, and even when they do, it is not altogether clear what sort of contribution they could make.

During more than twenty years in West Africa I was always absorbed in urgent practical work and preoccupied by continually having to meet all kinds of unforseen technical challenges. But throughout that time I was constantly being forced to pause, to admire, and to wonder at the arts produced in those apparently "primitive" villages; and to ask myself, How is it that as works of art they are so good? What makes their appeal so immediate, and so universal? What is the secret of their extraordinary *relevance* and their power to move us? The "something" in us which responds instinctively is surely not merely sentimentality or nostalgia. And anyway, if it is nostalgia, is that, after all, a discreditable feeling which we ought to repress? Perhaps rather, what we call nostalgia is a strong but insistent voice (like the prompting of conscience) to which we should listen; if we refuse, then later on we shall be sorry that we were so deaf.

I kept asking myself, What is it they have but we have lost and which we feel we need so much? And why is it that in Europe, artists are a peculiar or special sort of person, operating outside the main stream, whereas there, almost everybody seems to be some kind of artist? There are some parts of West Africa where in almost any village there are people who can make beautiful carved stools, or woven cotton, or pots: not just one or two making good ones and the others making bad ones, but practically all of them—though naturally even there, some are better than others.

During that time I was unable to form any coherent or satisfying theory about it, until in 1968 I had the good fortune to be invited to participate in a project aimed at introducing pottery to the Aborigines in the Northern Territory of Australia. This brief, six-months experience gave me a new light on the question, because the Australian Aborigines are an *extreme case*. For tens of thousands of years they were without contacts with the rest of the world and their material culture was (perhaps in consequence of that isolation) the most rudimentary in the world. They had remained nomadic hunters and food-gatherers, with no agriculture, no art of building, no domesticated animals (except dogs) and of course no pottery. But their inner life and their rituals and mythology are rich with things we have forgotten about or else have allowed to become atrophied; and they always produced good art, though the range was limited.

At that point I remembered what someone had written about children: "the world-wide fraternity of children is the greatest of savage tribes and the only one which shows no signs of dying out"; and I also reflected that up to a certain age practically all children are good primitive artists.

From the moment of birth a child is destined to be an artist. "Into the dangerous world I leapt"—a world also full of goodness and reassurance, what we call love. The love because of the danger, presumably; but in any case an exciting and significant world. A child has not got the techniques and the means of expression which we subsequently acquire; but being aware that the world is overflowing with some tremendous significance he has to do something—or rather make something—as a kind of acknowledgement of the mystery. He does it by *making certain things mean something*, by giving esoteric names, properties and meanings to certain stones, sticks, trees, animals or places. He invests them with a kind of supernatural significance and potency, composes highly subjective stories or songs about them and expresses his convictions by drawing, painting, constructing, or by some kind of dance.

But in the West, as children grow older they have to be educated for a certain kind of civilisation, and most of them become so interested in learning all the tricks which that civilisation expects of them, that they abandon their primeval art-faculty and it never grows beyond the embryonic stage.

Luckily for us there are always a few who for some reason do not allow that to happen. I wonder what the reason is: were they specially happy in childhood, or specially unhappy? Whatever the reason, they find that all the tricks they learn at school—for instance how to read and write by manipulating those bloodless, abstract phonetic bricks which we call the letters of the alphabet—all these accomplishments they find to be unsatisfactory in some way because they are not the right medium for expressing what they want to express, or rather what they know must somehow be expressed. This is not necessarily because they are less clever than the other children in ordinary school subjects; it is more likely that they are rather less easily satisfied. Whatever the cause, it is these, or some of them, who later on become artists. They have refused to allow their primitive, pre-logical faculties to stop dead at the embryonic stage, and insist on discovering for themselves some technical channel through which they can express their wordless inner convictions and communicate them to others in an acceptable, intelligible form—such as pots. In a word, the artist *as artist*—that is, when he is doing his thing and not pretending to be a professor or a technician or a man of business—obtains his stuff from the same sources as a child or an aboriginal tribesman.

For this reason I would maintain that all art is in a sense primitive, and define a "primitive" culture as one in which, to a much greater extent than with us, people have managed to keep open their life-lines to the hidden sources of art. If by some extraordinary good fortune a Western potter has the opportunity to work with such people, his relationship with them, totally unlike that of a teacher of "Western" subjects like mathematics or literature, does not depend on words and is not impeded by the barriers of language. Words in themselves, quite apart from any difficulties of translation, are a kind of "trap"; they can easily become masks enabling human beings to hide from each other instead of communicating. When people are working together "on the level", at the same work, a more immediate kind of understanding grows up between them. The difficulties, and the pleasures, of the work do not need the medium of language in order to be shared, and what you have in common comes into action, bypassing the divisive effect of words and the sometimes disastrous misunderstandings to which they can give rise. The work you are doing together, the stuff you are using and the things you are making, are universal and belong to everyone. You are returning to the concrete thing itself. You take a new look at that simple idea—the unity of the human race—which up till then was only an idea in your mind, and find that it is now taking a practical shape. You begin at least to feel the reality of the fact that all human beings are essentially the same.

There is another benefit which a Western potter will get in such a situation. Making pottery in primitive conditions presents him with a continual series of technical challenges, and these have a bracing effect on his own potting, since the effort to overcome technical problems and difficulties is an integral part of the *content*, the expression which he puts into his work, not something separate or different in kind. Absorbed in the struggle with natural and technical obstacles he will be tasting some of the exhilarations, as well as the frustrations, of one who is exploring new paths in his art, and this restores to him a way of working which makes it possible, as never before, to make good pots. His instinct for expression, or creation, returns to where it belongs—to the subconscious part of his being, where it will function much better because it is not continually interfered with by the busy, anxious meddling of what we are pleased to call The Mind. He will find himself making pots as naturally as a tree makes leaves or fruits—which is the way the village potters make theirs. This also is a large part of what I mean when I say, rather inarticulately, that during my years in West Africa I constantly found that I was receiving far more than I could give.

A Western potter may get a lot of illumination by working in primitive conditions, but do primitive potters really need him? The only reason that makes me think the answer can perhaps be a cautious "Yes" is that primitive arts are mortally threatened by the impact of Western civilisation—an impact which is inevitable, whether he happens to be there or not. Sometimes a craft may die out altogether, to be superseded by something else. This is sad, but the same thing has often happened to our traditional crafts in the West. It is the price which sometimes has to be paid for material progress, and primitive villagers, quick to appreciate the advantages of the progress, do not mind paying the price. Unlike us they are not sentimentalists, and we, who have never experienced the toughness of their primary poverty, are not in a position to say they are wrong. But usually what happens is something far worse. Traders arrive in the village and decide that there is money to be made out of all this beauty: the craft is valued, but valued for the wrong reasons. Instead of being allowed to lapse (if that is its natural fate), it is deliberately diverted and debased to meet a foreign and basically *profane* market. The craftsman, needing the money, becomes a willing tool in his own degradation, and at the end of the process (there are sorts of half-way stages along the road) he is producing mere imitations of the real thing. The craft continues to exist, but in a horrible kind of *zombie* existence, long after its real life has been extinguished. The craftsman is betrayed into making a "trap to catch tourists", where formerly what he made was a depository of the soul.

This process is going on everywhere, in Europe, America, Asia, Africa, Australia, even in the Arctic Circle; and evidently the world being what it is, it is not going to stop. We ("the enlightened") are continually deploring it, but our deploring is always ineffectual. We ought to be doing something about it instead of wringing our hands like useless spectators. Already in certain places the real artists of the country are doing something—for instance in West Africa; and some of them will call it paternalistic presumption on our part if we also try to help. But I say there is work (not necessarily the same work) for the outsiders as well as for the insiders, and we should support one another.

Attempting to preserve a craft, even if successful, would only ensure a sort of glass-case survival. The aim should rather be to facilitate a healthier, more progressive kind of development—adaptation or transition—this being what normally takes place when changes in the environment or in the style of living threaten a craft with obsolescence. A historical example of this process of transition is afforded by what happened with European potters when Chinese porcelain first arrived on the Western scene. In technique, porcelain is vastly superior to the lead-glazed earthenware of medieval Europe, but this did not cause our native potters in the seventeenth and eighteenth centuries to give up potting, or to take refuge in a "Souvenir trade". Instead, they gradually developed their techniques in response to the new challenge. First they adopted tin-glaze from the Moslem world and began to make their first attempts to imitate the imported porcelain; and eventually, after a long history of technical advances, they found out how to make the real thing. But however carefully they imitated, the native European character was always coming through, without any conscious cult of their own ancestral styles—as it always will if it has vitality to begin with.

This is not an exact parallel, and I am not trying to suggest that every stage of European evolution must necessarily be repeated in other places; but the thought of the successful transition which our potters made in that period sustained me in Nigeria in my belief that if I could somehow contrive a situation which would provide my pupils with the right chance, they also would make a similar transition and produce pots which would be as appropriate to their new ways of life as the traditional ware had been (and still in many places is) for the life-style of the villages.

I wonder now whether a happy situation like that will ever occur again, and whether in the future a Western potter will ever get the chance to participate in that kind of work. The world is now divided into the Old Rich Nations and the Young Poor Nations, and the latter have learnt a lot in the past few hundred years—among other things, to "fear the Greeks even when they come with gifts in their hands".

They might also invoke, against anyone who aspired to work in that way, a formidable engine, which may be called The Better-Dead Argument. It goes something like this: "If the old folk-arts are doomed to be debased and humiliated as Native Curios or Airport Art, it is really better that people should be allowed to get on with it without interference. Any art—any *particular* art—can die out, and in fact has to die out eventually in the course of nature. But art itself, the art impulse, the style or genius of a people does not and cannot die. It may go underground for a season but eventually it will come out again in some new and healthy form. This is a law of nature, and we should not meddle with it. It is futile and sentimental to resist the forces which are debasing our traditional arts, and anything you do will sooner or later succumb to those forces."

The argument sounds very strong, but I refuse to be intimidated by it. It is nothing but the voice of Voltaire's Doctor Pangloss, who was always maintaining in the face of the worst disasters that "all is for the best in this best of all possible worlds". Certainly you cannot extinguish a people's genius. But there have been plenty of occasions in history when Western Man came as near as he possibly could to doing just that, and no "Doctor Pangloss" is going to persuade me that it was a good thing, or anything but an unspeakable loss and grief, for us as well as for the victims. One example, still painfully relevant, was the West African Slave Trade, which meant an absolute and total disinheritance, deprivation and loss for the slaves, while for us and everybody else, what was done then has left a legacy which is still acting as a pervading poison, and it is difficult to see how Western Man is ever going to settle the account.

It might be maintained that in place of their lost potential for happiness—the family lives, ethnic traditions and ancestral arts of the slaves—their descendants achieved a great moral power, and that this is of more value than any art or craft or even than happiness itself. But this is an argument which human beings (so long at least as they are guided by the light of nature) are not entitled to use, not being competent to judge the balance of loss or gain in such tremendous matters; we do not possess the scales in which to weigh them. But there are some things of which we are not only competent to judge but in fact are obliged by our nature to judge: these are the data of ethics, and of aesthetics. Ethics is about our duties to our neighbour; but aesthetics is about our duties to all the things and creatures of the world we belong to. Our aesthetic conscience is therefore just as tender and just as imperious as the ethical conscience. Anyone who has felt the value—that is, *the meaning*—of primitive arts feels also that we must try to do something to defend them, because they are necessities, not just academic curiosities. We need them, not as dead specimens, but as things which have the power to make us grow and change and to nourish us in the future.

And *it could just be* that modern craftsmen in the West are more likely to know about this than anyone else, simply because we experienced a very long time ago the sense of what was lost when we had to circumscribe our primitive art-faculty and allow it to wither away. The other races, who are still enjoying the full use of it, will feel the same sensation of irreparable loss after they in turn have let theirs die—as might well happen. But by then it will be too late; and when they find out what they have lost they will blame us, because it was our civilisation which made them lose it and because we failed to act at the critical time. We were afraid of being called paternalist and were too ready to agree that we were not our brothers' keepers.

Surely we and they can agree that the best hope for primitive crafts is to aim at some kind of transition; to keep the primitive art instinct alive by making a modern channel for it. If a Western craftsman ever again gets the opportunity to take part in that work, he will be helping to look after something tender, vulnerable and very precious, nursing it like a naked baby through the crisis of transition, into the new world which is waiting for it. If he also has the chance to persevere in it until he can feel some confidence that the baby is really going to survive, then in at least one small area the Fatal Impact would not be fatal, and might even be called a fertilising contact.

Michael Cardew

BIBLIOGRAPHY

BOOKS

Brears, Peter C. D. *The English Country Potter*. Newton Abbot: David and Charles, 1971.

Cardew, Michael A. *Pioneer Pottery*. London: Longman, 1969; New York: St. Martin's Press, 1971.

Casson, Michael. *Pottery in Britain Today*. London: Tiranti, 1967.

Cooper, Ronald C. *English Slipware Dishes 1650–1850*. London: Tiranti, 1968.

Digby, G. R. Wingfield. *The Work of the Modern Potter in England*. J. Murray: London, 1952.

Hennell, Thomas. *The Countryman at Work*. London: Architectural Press, 1947.

Hettes, Karel, and Rada, Pravoslav. *Modern Ceramics*. London: Drury House, 1965.

Holland, William Fishley. *Fifty Years a Potter*. London: *Pottery Quarterly* special publication, 1958.

Honey, William B. *Art of the Potter*. London: Faber, 1946.

Leach, Bernard. *A Potter's Book* (Preface by Michael Cardew). London: Faber, 1940; New York: Transatlantic, 1965.

Leith Ross, Sylvia. *Nigerian Pottery* (Introduction by Michael Cardew). Ibadan University Press, 1970.

Rose, Muriel. *The Artist Potter in England*. London: Faber, 1955.

PERIODICALS

Cardew, Michael A. "Industry and the Studio Potter". *Crafts* 2 (1942), The Red Rose Guild of Craftsmen.

————. "Bernard Leach". *The Studio*, November 1925.

————. "Pioneer Pottery at Abuja". *Nigeria Quarterly* 52 (1956).

————. "Bernard Leach: Recollections". *Essays in Appreciation of Bernard Leach* (*New Zealand Potter* special issue), 1960.

————. "A View of African Pottery". *Ceramic Monthly*, February 1974.

————. "Ladi Kwali". *Craft Horizons*, April 1972.

————. "Why I Make Pots". *Ceramic Review* 33 (May-June 1975).

————. Review of "International Ceramics 1972" exhibition. *Ceramic Review* 17 (October 1972).

————. "Pottery in Northern Nigeria". *Pottery Quarterly* 3 (1956).

————. "Training Potters at Abuja". *Pottery Quarterly* 10

————. "Firing the Big Pot at Kwali". *Nigeria Quarterly* 70 (September 1961).

————. "Australian Aborigines as Potters". *Pottery Quarterly*.

————. "Potters and Amateur Potters". *Pottery Quarterly* 10 (1971). (Similar to monograph with same title published by the National Council on Education for the Ceramic Arts, USA).

————. "Design". *Currency* (magazine of the Australian Reserve Bank), July 1969.

Counts, Charles. "Michael Cardew". *Craft Horizons*, February 1972.

Marsh, Ernest. "Michael Cardew: A Potter of Winchcombe, Gloucestershire". *Apollo*, March 1943.

O'Brien, Michael. "Abuja after Michael Cardew". *Ceramic Review* 34 (July-August 1975).

Pleydell-Bouverie, Katharine. "At St. Ives in the Early Years". *Essays in Appreciation of Bernard Leach* (*New Zealand Potter* special issue), 1960.

————. "Michael Cardew: A Personal Account". *Ceramic Review* 20 (March-April 1973).

"Michael Cardew and Associates". *Crafts*, July-August 1975.

MONOGRAPHS AND CATALOGUES

Cardew, Michael A. *A Preliminary Survey of Pottery in West Africa*. Department of Commerce and Industry, Lagos, 15 September 1950.

————. *Potters and Amateur Potters*. National Council on Education for the Ceramic Arts, U.S.A. 4 pages.

————. *Life as a Potter*. American Crafts Council Southeast Workshop, Arrowmont School, Gatlinburg, Tennessee, June 1971. 11 pages.

————. *Stoneware Pottery*. Catalogue of Cardew exhibition. London, Berkeley Galleries, November 1950.

————. *Stoneware Pottery*. Catalogue of exhibition of Cardew work at Abuja. London, Berkeley Galleries, February-March 1958.

————. *Stoneware Pottery*. Catalogue of exhibition of work by Cardew and his pupils at Abuja. London, Berkeley Galleries, September-October 1959.

————. *Stoneware Pottery*. Catalogue of exhibition of work by Cardew and his pupils at Abuja. London, Berkeley Galleries, June-July 1962.

Leach, Bernard; Cardew, Michael; Houston, John, et al. *Michael Cardew: A Collection of Essays*. London: Crafts Advisory Committee, 1976.

FILMS

Pottery in the Gold Coast. 1944.

Pottery in Abuja. Alister Hallum, 1965.

Mud and Water Man. Alister Hallum, Arts Council of Great Britain, 1974.

INDEX

Aborigines, Australian, 83, 84, 216, 217
Abuci, 211, 213
Abuja, 59, 60, 73–78, 82, 91, 201, 202, 209–213
Achimota College, 40, 43, 44, 47, 57, 82, 204, 205
Agbedanu, Kwami, 207
Alajo Pottery, 43–47, 204–207
"Amateur and Professional Potters", 111
America, 83, 89
Arrowmont School, 76, 89
Ashbee Guilds, 43
Attey, Kofi, 48, 77, 90, 110, 207, 209
Bauhaus, 46
Benson, Kent, 83, 110
Bergen, Henry, 37, 109
Berkley Gallery, 53, 76
Beyer, Svend, 81, 82, 110
Bosch, Sias, 110
Braden, Norah, 21
Braunton Pottery, 11, 13, 16, 199
Brears, Peter, 30
Brygos Gallery, 37
Cardew, Alexandra, 12
Cardew, Arthur, 11, 12
Cardew, Cornelius, 37
Cardew, Ennis, 37
Cardew, Mariel, 37, 40, 53, 74
Cardew, Philip, 53
Cardew, Seth, 37, 111
clay(s), 73, 198, 201, 203, 205–208, 211, 213
Comfort, Elijah, 31, 32, 198, 199
Commerce and Industry Department, Nigeria, 57, 60
Cooper, Ronald, 29
Counts, Charles, 90
Craftsman Potters Association, 110
Davis, Harry, 40, 44, 204–206
Dicks, Peter, 110

Digby, George Wingfield, 48, 99
Dunn, George, 15, 197
earthenware, 48, 81
Fagg, Bernard, 77
"The Fatal Impact", 98, 215–224
Fieldhouse, Murray, 197
Finch, Raymond, 38–40, 110, 199
Fishley, Edwin Beer, 11, 12, 16
Fremington Pottery, 12, 16, 31, 32
Fry, Roger, 15
Gboko, Peter, 213
Geology for Potters course, 82
German Craft Guilds, 46
Gill, Eric, 90
glaze(s), 48, 53, 73, 74, 199, 201–203
Greenslade, Sydney, 109
Greet Pottery, 25, 198, 199
Gropius, Walter, 46
Hallum, Alister, 91
Hamada, Shōji, 13–16, 23, 95, 100, 111, 197
Hammond, Henry, 82
Hennell, Thomas, 109
Hockney, David, 98
Holland, Fishley, 11, 13, 31
Husani, 213
Ido, Isibi, 213
"Industry and the Studio Potter", 45
International Ceramics Exhibition, 1972, 81, 98
Ismay, William, 109
Jos Museum, 72, 209
Jos Plateau, 73, 212, 213
Karo, Abu, 213
Kennedy, Margaret, 23
Kenzan, 14
kilns, 31, 32, 39, 40, 48, 73, 197, 199, 200, 206, 207, 209–211
Kitchin, G. W., 12
Kwali, Ladi, 59, 74–77, 90, 213

Leach, Bernard, 11–16, 21–25, 44, 76, 95, 99,100, 109, 197

Leach Pottery, 15, 76, 197

Mackenzie, Compton, 60

Marcks, Gerhard, 43

Marsh, Ernest, 38

Martin, Wallace, 11

Matsubayashi, Tsuranosuke, 16, 21, 22, 24, 45, 197

McCormick, Thelma, 90

McMeekin, Ivan, 53, 83, 110, 201

Meyerowitz, H. V., 43, 46, 47, 75, 205

Milner-White, Eric, 109

Moorcroft, 14

Moorhead, Alan, 215

Morgan, William de, 11

Morris, William, 43

Mud and Water Man, 91

Muhtari, Ibrahim, 213

Murray, Keith, 44

Murray, William Staite, 11, 44

Muthesius, Hermann, 43

Naanabi, 213

Naylor, Gillian, 98

New Zealand, 83

Nupé potters, 58

O'Brien, Michael (Seamus), 82, 110, 111

Pioneer Pottery, 16, 82, 83, 110

Pleydell-Bouverie, Katherine (Beano), 16, 21, 22, 24, 38, 48, 82, 97, 197

"A Preliminary Study of Pottery in West Africa", 59

Pyker, Tod, 110

Rabinowitz, Hym, 81, 110

Raku ware, 24

Riemerschmidt, 109

Rose, Muriel, 37, 53, 99

Rosenthal, Philip, 77

Rothenstein, Sir Henry, 21

Rothschild, Henry, 109

Royal Institute Galleries, 37

Russell, Gordon, 44

slipware, 16, 23, 25, 29, 30, 81, 99

Smithsonian Institution, 90, 98

Staffordshire pottery, 30, 45

St. Ives, 13–16, 21–24, 82, 99, 100, 197, 199

Stoke-on-Trent, 22, 31, 37, 40, 44, 45

stoneware, 24, 48, 53, 81

Tafewa, Ababaker, 73

Tanko, 213

Taylor, Howson, 14

Toft, Thomas, 25, 30

Tomimoto, Kenkichi, 14

Toto, Lami, 213

Tustin, Charlie, 37, 198

Tustin, Sidney, 32, 37, 40, 198, 199

Ushafa, Bawa, 75, 213

Ushafa, Kande, 213

University of Wisconsin, 83

Van de Velde, Henry, 43

Victoria and Albert Museum, 37, 53, 81–82, 99

Vumé Dugamé, 46–48, 53, 77, 91, 111, 202, 207–210

Vyse, Charles, 14

Warhol, Andy, 98

Wells, Reginald, 14

Wenford Bridge Pottery, 39, 40, 53, 78, 81–84, 89–92, 200–203, 210

Winchcombe Pottery, 25, 29–32, 37–40, 48, 77, 81, 99, 109, 110, 198–200, 210

Woolf, Virginia, 15

Yanagi, Sōetsu, 14, 78

Yoruba potters, 58